Let It Rot!

The Gardener's Guide to Composting

STU CAMPBELL

Storey Books
Schoolhouse Road
Pownal, Vermont 05261

The mission of Storey Communications is to serve our customers by publishing practical information that encourages personal independence in harmony with the environment.

Edited by Kathleen Bond Borie
Cover design by Meredith Maker
Cover photograph by Kevin Kennefick
Text design by Meredith Maker and Erin Lincourt
Production by Susan Bernier and Erin Lincourt
Line drawings on pages iv, 1, 5, 11, 13, 16, 20, 25, 29, 30, 33, 35, 37, 43, 45, 47, 84, 89, 94, 96, 101, 103, 106, 117, 121, 126, 129, 136, 140, 141, 142, and 145 by Jean Loewer, on pages 53, 65, 73, 85, 86, 93, 99, 119, 132, and 137 by Alison Kolesar, and on pages 67, 75, and 77 by Susan Berry Langsten
Indexed by Hagerty & Holloway

The information in this book is true and complete to the best of our knowledge. All recommendations are made without guarantee on the part of the author or Storey Communications, Inc. The author and publisher disclaim any liability in connection with the use of this information. For additional information please contact Storey Communications, Inc., Schoolhouse Road, Pownal, Vermont 05261.

Storey Books are available for special premium and promotional uses and for customized editions. For further information, please call the Custom Publishing Department at 800-793-9396.

Printed in the United States by R.R. Donnelley
10 9 8 7 6 5 4 3 2 1

Library of Congress Cataloging-in-Publication Data

Campbell, Stu.
 Let it rot! : the gardener's guide to composting / by Stu Campbell. — [3rd. ed.]
  p. cm. — (Storey's down-to-earth guides)
 Includes bibliographical references (p.) and index.
 ISBN 1-58017-023-4 (pbk. : alk. paper)
 1. Compost. I. Title. II. Series.
S661.C35 1998
631.8'75—dc21
               97-36405
               CIP

To Gregory
May he, like his father, have the chance
to pursue what interests him most.

Contents

"One aker well compast, is worth aker three . . . "

— Tusser (1557)

"Now I am terrified at the Earth, it is that calm
  and patient,
It grows such sweet things out of such corruptions,
It turns harmless and stainless on its axis, with
  such endless succession of diseased corpses,
It distills exquisite winds out of such infused fetor,
It gives such divine materials to men, and accepts
  such leavings from them at last."

— Walt Whitman, "This Compost"

Home Composting: Art or Science?

Somewhere, thousands and thousands of years ago, some hairy and slouched cave dwellers who groveled in the dirt with sticks and who managed to grow some food may have discovered that seeds grew better near the place where they piled the apparently useless refuse from their cave. Most of this "waste" material was organic matter.

I doubt very much that at the moment of discovery they had either the wisdom or the inclination to shout "Eureka!" But they must have passed the word along, because the idea of putting human, animal, vegetable, and mineral wastes on or into the soil, to make it better, spread to all corners of the world.

In the beginning, there was manure. Humanity has known for a long time that animal excrement is valuable stuff when it comes to growing things and has apparently always made efforts to save it. But shortly after early humans became friendly enough with animals to be able to persuade a few of them to live at home with them in a more or less peaceful relationship, they must have realized that there was never quite enough manure to go around. So they began to devise ways of stretching it and started to think about ways to make "synthetic manure." They didn't know what they were doing, really. They probably just took a look at what was going on and then began trying things. Composting had begun long before our ancestors discovered it.

Decomposition is at least as old as the soil. The earth itself, as the poet Walt Whitman suggests, is something of a compost pile. "It gives such divine materials to men, and accepts such leavings from them at last." Long before there were people around to observe it, composting was going on in every forest, every meadow, every swamp, and bog, and prairie, and steppe in the world. As Richard Langer says, "Composting is a natural process that began with the first plants on earth and has been going on ever since."

"Primitive" Composting

Ancient people were the true discoverers of organic gardening — in spite of whatever valid claims people like Sir Albert Howard or Rudolf Steiner or J. I. Rodale may have to the *modern* title. Whoever they were, they were artists, not scientists. Only by trial and error were they able to learn what worked when it came to making synthetic manure. They didn't have anyone to guide them or to give them good advice because there was nobody around who knew very much. Things like psychrophylic bacteria and the relationship between carbon and nitrogen in the process of decomposition were the furthest things from their minds — and at least thirty centuries away in terms of time.

All they saw, maybe, was the forest floor where leaves fell, turned dark, and gradually disappeared to be transformed into the dark, fertile soil gardeners were someday to call "humus." They must have realized that in time many things rot whether we try to do anything about it or not. Leave everything to Mother Nature, and eventually the conditions that encourage decay will establish themselves. We can be thankful that this is something that has been going on since shortly after the beginning of time.

"Modern" Composting

Allowing nature to take its course, however, may take more time than we have. *The modern practice of composting is little more than speeding up and intensifying natural processes.* That's *all* it is. When you come right down to it, finished compost is no more than "treated" or "predigested" (rotted) organic matter, which usually has undergone a natural heating process and which is very valuable stuff to incorporate into your garden's soil.

For too long there has been an air of cultist mysticism surrounding the art of composting. This is the kind of nonsense so many people find objectionable in a lot of composting literature. It is easy to get confused by gardening magazines and gardening books that describe the "science" of composting in such narrowly defined terms that you get the distinct impression that there is one, and *only* one, method for making humus.

Don't misunderstand: There have been all kinds of *extremely* valuable scientific research done on composting, and much of the information gathered can be very helpful to the home composter as well as to the municipality that is doing or considering composting on a large scale. I suggest that you try to learn as much about the highly technical aspects of the subject as you can. But I caution that an overly scientific approach to composting may take all the fun out of it.

The word *compost* comes from two Latin roots, *com* meaning "together," and *post*, meaning "to bring." To make edible "fruit compost" (or "fruit compote"), for example, is to bring together several different kinds of fruit, mix them with sugar and other ingredients in a jar or crock, and let it sit to ferment for several days. It really doesn't matter how long it sits or precisely how much you add of what. In fact, you might eat some of the mixture, and when the container gets low, replenish it with other fixings as they become available. The final concoction is almost always a delicious one, though rarely, if ever, the same as the last. There are really as many recipes for making fruit compote as there are fruit compote makers — probably more. You'll find the same is true with composting.

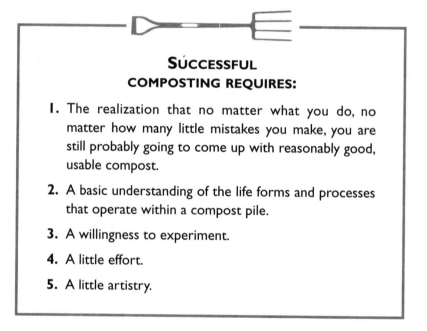

SUCCESSFUL
COMPOSTING REQUIRES:

1. The realization that no matter what you do, no matter how many little mistakes you make, you are still probably going to come up with reasonably good, usable compost.

2. A basic understanding of the life forms and processes that operate within a compost pile.

3. A willingness to experiment.

4. A little effort.

5. A little artistry.

As you get into composting, try not to get bogged down with complicated recipes and formulas. A few simple guidelines can help you eliminate some of the traditionally unpleasant aspects of composting. There are few hard-and-fast rules governing the making of good compost that must be followed to the letter.

If you are a beginner, start thinking in simple terms about a compost system. Later, you may want to develop more complicated and sophisticated techniques. Apply what scientific knowledge you have. If you find a particular section of the book too technical, skip it. You can always return to it at a later point.

Be creative. Select what you can from the information offered here and go on to establish your own composting style. When your neighbors tell you that you are doing it "all wrong," tell them that both of you are right. As you learn more and more about composting and begin to understand the rotting process a little better, you may grow to appreciate the recycling activity that takes place in nature day in and day out. You may also find, as others have, that you want to synchronize yourself with it.

Principle of Return

Composting is based on the principle of return, a principle by which all good organic gardeners try to live. But you don't have to be a purely organic gardener to be a composter. I have become more aware, sometimes with the help of organic gardening friends, that all of life is part of a continuous pattern, which should not be interrupted. As humans we reap things from the land in the form of produce. But this is only one small part of a much larger picture. There are many other life forms besides ours that come into play and help to make the cycle run. Giving *back* to the land is every bit as vital as taking *from* it. And we have taken too much for too long. Although we may never be able to offset the damage we have done to the soil and replace *all* that we have taken from it, it is not too late to try to make amends. Composting is a way of *using up* what we have in abundance — humble things like weeds and dead grass and garbage and old sticks — to repay a long-standing debt to the earth. By becoming more and more attuned to the mechanics of Mother Nature you realize that, as my friend Catharine Osgood Foster says in her book *Building Healthy Gardens*, "In the process of nature there is no throwing away."

My wife has often gently accused me of being a tightwad and a pack rat. She is probably right. I find it difficult to throw *anything* out — particularly anything that had its origin in some living thing and is potential compost material. Rather than argue with me, she has learned to throw out really worthless things when I'm not around, in the hope that I won't notice. I have told her over and over again that she should have realized when she decided to marry someone with a name like Stuart Duncan Campbell that he would probably turn out to be something of a thrifty soul. My Scottish heritage seems to make me a more natural composter than she, but she is gradually coming around to my way of thinking.

Serious composters tend to reach a point where they view most of the solid and liquid material in the world as falling into one of three categories: (1) desirable compostable stuff, (2) undesirable compostable stuff, and (3) nonbiodegradable stuff. I sometimes have to resist the urge to stop by the side of the road and gather up a particularly attractive bunch of leaves or cut weeds. While watching television a few evenings ago, I couldn't help but notice the beautiful clumps of kelp two lovers were treading on as they walked arm in arm along a California beach in some low-budget film. I found myself wondering if maybe our garden couldn't use a little boron and perhaps a touch of the iodine contained in seaweed. I then started wishing that I could have some of that kelp for my compost pile. I soon lost the thread of the plot and decided to go to bed. This kind of thing doesn't happen *all* the time, mind you.

The basic thread here is this: Let common sense and the organic materials that are most available to you be your number one and number two composting guides. After that, I hope *Let It Rot!* will be of some help.

Why Compost?

For years, Americans have been dumping millions of tons of household garbage into overflowing landfills without blinking, but today we are having to face facts: The capacity of landfills is finite, and the costs of maintaining them — economic, social, and environmental — are growing. Landfills are filling up at an alarming rate; twenty-three now ban yard trimmings and more are heading in that direction. But when we look at our ordinary household waste, we see that about three-fourths of it is composed of organic materials that can easily be composted instead. The volume of yard waste we generate works out to about 230 pounds per person per year. Food waste adds another 100 pounds per person per year. Multiply that by the number of people in your household and you begin to realize that composting can make a big difference. It's estimated that all residences could reduce their total annual volume of waste by 35 percent if they composted at home.

As we begin to reevaluate our throw away society, composting is looking increasingly attractive. Homeowners are disposing of their kitchen garbage and yard wastes in backyard compost piles, and municipal landfills are finding that large-scale composting is a cheaper, space-saving alternative. Compost is one solution to our solid-waste woes, and what's more, it offers gardeners and lawn keepers an invaluable source of soil nutrients. Let's take a look at what that crumbly end product can do for you.

Soil Health

First of all, as a gardener you already know that the key to healthy plants is healthy soil. No amount of fertilizer can make up for poor soil, nor will your plants be able to withstand the normal ravages of insects, disease, drought, wind, and other stresses if they don't have their roots in good soil. You are not just doing your plants a favor when you add compost to the soil, you are giving them sustenance.

Fortunately, compost is by definition a composite of different ingredients, some of which will rot more rapidly than others. This is good. Actually, if everything were to decompose at the same speed, the end product would not be so valuable. During the first year after application, about half of the compost breaks down in the soil and half of the nitrogen and sulfur is available to plants. Much of the calcium, magnesium, and potassium is also available. Yet because certain types of matter, such as lignin and cellulose, break down more slowly than others, nutrients will continue to be released over a long period of time.

Compost continues contributing to the garden soil even *after* all of the organic matter it contained has rotted away. Compost that is almost completely decomposed comes close to what Dr. Ehrenfried Pfeifer calls "stable humus." "Stability" implies that the substance can no longer break down rapidly, since the degradable organic matter as such has all but disappeared. From this point on, further decomposition must be very gradual. Now the large compounds are "locked up" in their microscopic bodies. Once the proper conditions of moisture, oxygen, and temperature are just right, *they* will start to decompose, and these organic compounds can be released into the soil.

Now that you're convinced you can't live without compost one more day, you're probably itching to get your hands dirty. First, it will help you to learn a little bit about what goes on inside the compost pile so yours will get off to a good start.

HOW COMPOST HELPS YOUR SOIL

- Compost contains nutrients that your plants need for optimum growth, such as nitrogen, phosphorus, and potassium. And it's an especially good supplier of micronutrients that are needed in small quantities and are sometimes overlooked by gardeners, such as boron, cobalt, copper, iodine, iron, manganese, molybdenum, and zinc. The more varied the materials used to make the compost, the greater the variety of nutrients your compost will provide. In some situations, you may not even need to fertilize soil enriched with compost.
- Nutrients are released at the rate your plants need them. In early spring, as your plants are slowly starting their growth, the microorganisms in compost are slowly releasing nutrients. As the weather warms up and your plants begin rapid growth, the microorganisms also work faster, releasing more food for your plants. Isn't nature wonderful?
- The organic matter in compost binds with soil particles (sand, silt, and clay) to form small aggregates, or crumbs. Crumbly soil is said to have good structure, as opposed to sand, which has poor structure because it's too coarse to form aggregates, or clay, which can act like cement when wet. These aggregates hold water on their surfaces, making it available to your plants as they need it. As aggregates form, more spaces are created for oxygen, an essential for good root

growth. At the same time, the soil spaces form channels for excess water to percolate through the soil, improving drainage.

- Increases water-holding capacity of soil. Compost can hold an amount of water equal to 200 percent of its dry weight, compared to 20 percent for a low-humus soil.
- Acts as an inoculant to your soil, adding microorganisms and larger creatures such as earthworms and insects, which are nature's soil builders. The compost environment is teeming with life, and all soils can benefit from such a rejuvenation.
- Neutralizes various soil toxins and metals, such as cadmium and lead, by bonding with them so they can't be taken up by plants.
- Acts as a pH buffer so plants are less dependent on a specific soil pH. The earthworms in the compost help in this process, because in passing organic matter through their bodies they modify the pH of the soil. And you can lower the pH of your soil by adding compost made from acidic raw materials, such as oak or beech leaves, sawdust, and pine needles.
- Can be used in a variety of ways in your lawn or garden — as a seed-starting medium, as a soil enhancer, as a side-dressing. (For more information on using compost in the garden, see chapter 11.)

How
Decomposition
Works

As a nation we seem to worship cleanliness — at least it would appear that way to anyone watching television for long. But at times we seem helpless to solve the problem of the massive pollution we have brought upon ourselves. Many of us live in squeamish horror of "germs" and "bugs," of "odor-causing bacteria," "wormy things," "rot," and the "fungus among us." So we spray our outdoors with insecticides and our indoors with disinfectants. Maybe the time has come for us to start being less compulsive about ridding our surroundings of worms, insects, and bacteria and to become more conscious of how they benefit us. Things might be better if we just *let them rot!*

Microorganisms

Let's begin by talking about composting's lowest common denominators: the organisms that make the miracle of decomposition possible. To do this, we have to discuss some of the most technical aspects of composting first. But, take heart!

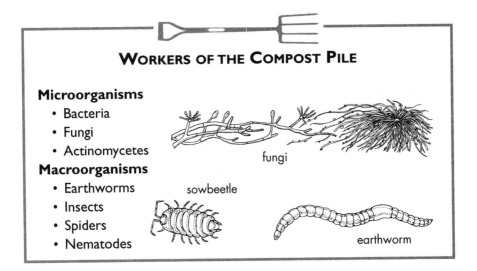

WORKERS OF THE COMPOST PILE

Microorganisms
- Bacteria
- Fungi
- Actinomycetes

fungi

Macroorganisms
- Earthworms
- Insects
- Spiders
- Nematodes

sowbeetle

earthworm

They are not as complicated as you might think. If you familiarize yourself with the terms mentioned here, you will be able to better understand why certain composting practices recommended later in the book should be followed.

One day I asked a friend, who holds a Ph.D. in microbiology (and he's a good gardener, too!), to sit down with me and explain a few things about the organisms that enable decomposition. I wanted him to tell me what *really* goes on under all those chopped leaves and hay in my compost pile. Here's what I learned:

Sir Albert Howard, the British organic horticulturist who did much to remind modern folks of the value of composting, tells us that living microorganisms (such as bacteria and fungi) too small for us to see — *not* human beings — are the agents that make compost. We'd be in big trouble if all microbial activity were suddenly to stop. Think of all the millions of tons of organic refuse produced in the world each day — the leaves, grass clippings, garbage, industrial waste, everything. Without tiny microorganisms to digest this refuse, not only would most of it stay around, but little carbon dioxide would be produced. Without carbon dioxide, plants can't grow.

In other words, without microorganisms there would be no decomposition, and the vital elements that are tied up in organic materials would never be released. All organic raw material, either left to rot on its own or put into a compost system, is in a crude form and contains substances that permit plants to grow. But it is in a state that makes these substances unavailable to them, which is why we need bacteria and fungi to do their work so that the nutrients locked up in vegetable and animal matter can be released. By continually digesting organics, microorganisms keep a constant flow of nutrients going to plants. In this sense, they are microscopic refineries, alchemists, and garbage collectors all rolled in to one.

What Microorganisms Need to Do Their Work

To grow and multiply, microorganisms need four things: (1) an energy source, or carbon; (2) a protein source, or nitrogen; (3) oxygen; and (4) moisture.

Carbon. Just as carbohydrates provide energy food for us, carbon provides the energy food for the microorganisms in your compost pile. We'll talk more about carbon materials in chapter 4, but basically they include dry, tough, fibrous plant materials like leaves, straw, sawdust, and cornstalks. Much of the bulky plant material from your yard and garden is high in carbon.

Nitrogen. Nitrogen materials provide the protein that microorganisms need in order to break down the carbon food. Nitrogen materials are considered activators in your compost pile because they get things cooking. Manure, grass clippings, green vegetation, blood meal, and kelp meal are some high-nitrogen materials. In general, they are not as fibrous and bulky as carbon materials and need to be added in smaller quantities.

It's helpful to think of the carbon materials as the food and the nitrogen materials as the digestive enzymes. Most of your organic matter should be high-carbon food with just enough nitrogen to help the microorganisms break down the carbon. If there's too little nitrogen, decomposition slows down. Excess nitrogen will be released as smelly ammonia gas.

Oxygen. Oxygen is required by many of the microorganisms, especially the most efficient bacteria, called *aerobes.* When not enough oxygen is available, the aerobes cannot survive and the *anaerobes* take over. Once this happens, decomposition slows by as much as 90 percent.

The aerobe can do a more complete job of composting than can the anaerobe. As the aerobe and its cohorts break down carbon compounds into carbon dioxide and water (which are immediately available to plants), they are also producing a lot of energy. This gives them a distinct advantage, because they can use this energy to grow that much faster themselves and decompose that much more material. At the same time, and no less important, they excrete plant nutrients such as nitrogen, phosphorus, and magnesium, to name just a few.

Meanwhile, back at the airtight heap, the anaerobes struggle to produce carbon dioxide, water, energy, and nutrients, too — although in much smaller quantities when compared to the aerobe's performance. They also produce a lot of useless organic acids and amines (ammonia-like substances), which are smelly, contain unavailable nitrogen, and in some cases are toxic to plants. Some of the end products of the anaerobe's efforts are hydrogen sulfide (which smells like rotten eggs), cadaverine, and putrescine. These last two descriptive names do a great deal to explain the nauseating odor of an anaerobic compost pile. So you see why this book places so much emphasis on keeping the pile well aerated.

Moisture. Moisture is necessary for soil creatures to do their work. Too little moisture slows decomposition; too much forces out the air, suffocating the most efficient microorganisms. The optimal moisture content is about 45 to 50 percent. We'll talk more about how to maintain adequate moisture in your pile in chapter 9.

Bacteria

There are thousands of different kinds of bacteria at work in a compost pile, but you need only be concerned with three main groups: psychrophiles, mesophiles, and thermophiles.

Psychrophiles

The first wave of microbial invasion into a compost pile may be by cool-temperature aerobic bacteria called *psychrophiles*. They do their best work at around 55°F, not far above refrigeration temperature. They attack the organic matter and start releasing nutrients in the form of amino acids.

When these microbes start digesting carbon compounds, the carbon is literally burned, or *oxidized*. Part of this oxidative energy is given off in the form of heat. In fact, heat is the by-product of any bacterial metabolism, but, contrary to what many people believe, it plays no part in the actual breaking down of organic matter. A rise in temperature, either as a result of intense bacterial activity inside the pile or as the result of higher atmospheric temperature outside the pile, will introduce different strains of organisms that grow most efficiently in this warmer climate. Any change in temperature, moisture content, or a dozen other conditions usually means that different microbes are going to show up.

Mesophiles

The second invasion, then, would be by a general category of bacteria called *mesophiles*. Most of the decomposition that takes place in a compost pile is

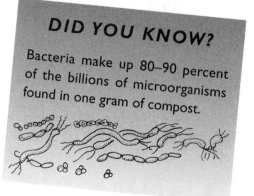

DID YOU KNOW?

Bacteria make up 80–90 percent of the billions of microorganisms found in one gram of compost.

mesophilic. Some microbiologists have gone so far as to say that mesophiles are as efficient as — or even more efficient than — their higher-temperature cousins usually associated with successful composting. This means that if your pile does not get extremely hot, decomposition is still taking place at a pretty good rate. The only problem posed by a failure to reach a high temperature is that disease-causing organisms and weed seeds are not so easily killed at mesophilic temperatures.

Mesophiles are comfortable at about the same temperature you and I are — around 70 to 90°F. In fact, if you were to start a compost pile in July when the temperature was consistently within this range, mesophiles would take over right away, and the psychrophilic process would be eliminated.

But don't be misled. A compost pile can be started any time. Fall is the time when most materials are readily available to gardeners. The period from the middle of November to about the middle of April, here in Vermont at least, is the time of the least microbial activity. But there is still some action. Because psychrophiles operate at such low temperatures (they are still effective at 28°F), decomposition takes place even in wintertime, although very slowly. Psychrophiles are very tenacious. Ice cream in a deep freeze will show a gradual increase in bacterial population, even though it may be months before the population will actually double.

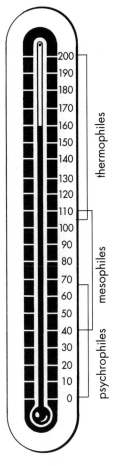

Each of the three main groups of bacteria operates at a different range of temperatures.

Thermophiles

If mesophiles generate too much heat they work themselves right out of a hospitable environment. The usually accepted line of demarcation between mesophilic and thermophilic activity is about 100°F. The thermophiles then take over and raise the temperature to about 160°, where it usually stabilizes. Some composters expect the pile to remain at this temperature peak for a sustained period of time and are disappointed when it returns to somewhere near the normal atmospheric temperature. In most cases, unless a pile is constantly fed new materials, carefully monitored, and turned at strategic times, the highest-range temperatures will last from three to five days only. But this is long enough for the thermophiles to perform their function. A gradual drop in temperature is not necessarily a sign that the compost is complete, nor an indication that the pile has become inactive. It merely indicates that the thermophiles have completed their work. It is now time for the mesophiles to come back into play.

Any one of these three types of microorganisms will continue metabolizing organic matter either until it is replaced by some other microbe or until there is nothing left to consume. At that point, they might die from lack of oxygen, or they might become inactive or die because there is no more carbon or nitrogen. Whenever bacteria die off in large numbers or take on the form of inactive spores, it is usually because all the available nutrients have been released and bacterial decomposition, for the most part, is complete.

> **DID YOU KNOW?**
>
> Thermophiles, which are common in manure, were originally found in the hot springs of Yellowstone National Park.

Fungi and Actinomycetes

While bacteria enact their changing of the guard and go about performing their various transformations of materials, there are other forms of life at work. Cool-temperature fungi, for instance,

Enzymes

Enzymes are substances produced by the bacteria. Their actual role in decomposition is a source of minor debate among microbiologists, but one thing about them is clear: They remain in the compost long after their parent bacteria have died off. While the bacteria are alive, the enzymes apparently assist in breaking down complex carbohydrates into simpler forms, which the bacteria can use as food. For instance, cellulose enzymes attack cellulose, which in most vegetable materials is quite resistant to rot. These enzymes help the fungi and actinomycetes that are trying to accomplish the same thing. What is most interesting is that they continue working away at the cellulose and lignin long after the microorganisms that produced them have died and become just another part of the compost.

start breaking down tough cellulose and lignin along with the psychrophilic bacteria. Thermophilic fungi usually appear in the pile four to six days after the pile has been constructed.

Actinomycetes have been described as "half-breed organisms" — part bacteria, part fungus — that operate at medium temperatures or in the moderate heat zones of the pile. When the pile is very hot near its core, they, like earthworms and mesophilic fungi, will work around the outer fringe. In large clusters, they are easy to spot and become most evident during the later stages of decomposition.

As you look inside your pile, you may notice a grayish "cobwebby" look among some of the fibrous material there. These are actinomycetes, and they ought not to be confused with the pale green mold that is a sign of an oxygenless condition in a compost heap. Actinomycetes give nearly finished compost a pleasing earthy smell. Anaerobic mold has a very different and distinct odor which, I assure you, you will recognize immediately as anything but pleasant.

In many ways the fungi and actinomycetes do the dirty work, cleaning up after the bacteria, consuming what they leave behind. They decompose the very toughest things: the remaining cellulose, starches, protiens, and lignin. Given a chance, they will even rot paper, which because it is made largely of lignin, is very difficult to break down.

Macroorganisms

Not all decomposition is microbiological. Just so you don't get the wrong impression, some mention should be made of the *macroorganisms* — the creatures you can see. These include earthworms, mites, grubs, insects, spiders, and nematodes. They dig, chew, digest, and mix compostable materials. Insects, of course, eat organic matter and increase the surface area for the bacteria and fungi to get at by chewing it into smaller pieces. Their excrement also is digested by bacteria, causing more nutrients to be released.

Earthworms

Any discussion of decomposition would be incomplete without mentioning the earthworm. Earthworms also ingest and digest organic matter. An earthworm eating its way through a compost pile passes organic matter through its body, grinding it with the help of tiny stones in its gizzard, and leaves dark, fertile, granular "castings" behind. A worm can produce its weight in castings each day. These granules are rich in plant nutrients that might otherwise be unavailable to plants. (We'll talk more about worm composting in chapter 6.)

Earthworms also seem to have a symbiotic relationship with bacteria. They do a lot of digesting for the bacteria, and the bacteria do a lot of digesting for them and provide food themselves. As earthworms eat decaying matter, they also take in and metabolize many of these microorganisms. My microbiologist friend says, "A worm is like a cow grazing on a field of bacteria. A bacterium is an unbelievably nutritious organism . . . fat-free . . . 60 percent protein." The presence of earthworms in either compost or soil is evidence of good microbial activity.

As you can see, in building a compost pile you are doing a great deal more than making something useful out of something apparently worthless, although that alone is gratifying enough. You are also creating a microcommunity, the population and character of which will be constantly changing and self-adjusting. You are initiating a series of events and conditions over which shortly you will have only minimal control. This can be an awesome thought if you have no knowledge of the governing system of checks and balances that nature — not you — establishes within the pile.

Once the micro- and macrobiological machinery is set in motion, all you can do is sit back and observe, intervening only when major things like the oxygen content and moisture content of the pile need some attention. If you feel somewhat god like as you first create your little universe in your backyard, your growing astonishment at the scope and speed of what is happening will replace whatever feelings of power you may have with real humility.

In comparison to man, microorganisms are titans if allowed to exist in any kind of favorable environment. The more you understand about what they do and what they need, the more you can help them. And the more you'll benefit from the fruits of their hard labor in the compost pile.

4

Compostable Materials Are All Around You

I used to worry about people who complained that they could never find enough organic matter to keep their garden soil in good shape, let alone accumulate enough to build a compost pile. That does *seem* like a problem in some particularly neat and well-kept city and suburban areas, but I don't worry so much any more. As Beatrice Trum Hunter points out in *Gardening Without Poisons*, "Our industrialized society has created a far greater variety of organic materials than ever existed previously." And as someone else once said, "Where there's a will, there's a way."

In some cases, you may have to seek out cheap sources of compostable material that you can *buy*. The point is that if you spend a little time looking, organic matter is easy to find.

Chances are that you will accumulate much of the same kinds of material all at once: leaves, or hay, or grass clippings.

If you put a lot of dry hay on your pile without mixing it with something else, you may create a situation in which you have too much carbonaceous material and not enough nitrogen in the pile. (The relationship between carbon and nitrogen is explained in detail later in this chapter.) Too many grass clippings will heat up all right, but they will probably form a slimy, anaerobic mess. Too many leaves all at once will mat. As you gather organic materials, leave part of what you gather *off* the pile, but somewhere nearby, so that you can mix it with whatever materials you may pick up later.

As a composter, you should not only have some knowledge of the biological processes taking place within the pile, you should also know something about the organic ingredients you are putting into your mixture. The greater the variety of things in the pile, the better. This variety increases the chances of obtaining a nicely balanced compost. The more diversified the mix, the more types of microorganisms will be at work.

It is possible that in a carefully controlled experimental situation, compost could be made according to precisely measured formulas, so that exactly the same compost is made over and over again. Under most ordinary circumstances, however, this is unnecessary. In fact, to my mind it is more fun to take potluck. If you are a novice, you may want to stick close to the standard but flexible rule of thumb for composting: two parts vegetable matter (grass, leaves, straw, etc.) to one part animal matter (manure).

The supply of compostable materials is limitless. To be composted, a material need only have two characteristics: (1) it must be biodegradable and (2) it must contain things that are usable and available to microorganisms. An incomplete listing of such things is on the next page.

A SIMPLE GUIDE

Compost = two parts vegetable matter (grass, leaves, straw) + one part animal matter (manure)

MATERIALS FOR YOUR COMPOST PILE

Alfalfa meal and hay

Algae (pond weeds)

Apple pomace (cider press waste)

Ashes (wood, not coal)

Buckwheat hulls or straw

Cocoa hulls

Cat litter (unused)

Citrus wastes

Clover

Coffee wastes and grounds

Corn cobs and stalks (shred or chop)

Cottonseed hulls

Cotton waste

Cowpeas

Dog food (dry food is nitrogen activator)

Dolomite

Earthworms

Eelgrass

Eggshells (grind or crush)

Flowers

Fruit peels

Grape pomace (winery waste)

Granite dust

Grass clippings

Greensand

Hay

Hedge clippings

Hops (brewery waste)

Kelp (seaweed)

Leaf mold

Leaves

Oat straw

Olive residues

Peanut hulls

Peat moss

Phosphate rock

Pine needles

Potash rock

Rhubarb leaves

Rice hulls

Shells (ground clam, crab, lobster, mussel, and oyster)

Sod

Soybean straw

Sphagnum moss

Sugarcane residue

Tea leaves

Vegetable peels and stalks

Vetch

Weeds

Wheat straw

Commonly Used Materials

It is not within the scope of this book to discuss in detail each of the items described below, but it is worth mentioning some of the things you are most likely to get your hands on without spending a great deal of time and money. These might include ashes, feathers, garbage, grass clippings, ground stone and shells, hedge trimmings, hops, leaves, leather waste, newspaper, peat moss, pine needles, sawdust, seaweed, sod, and weeds, among others.

Ashes

Coal ashes can be toxic to plants, but wood ashes from a fireplace or stove are valuable to any gardener, especially if they are sifted through a screen to get rid of large particles of charcoal. Wood ashes are a source of potash, or potassium carbonate. Some organic gardeners use ashes as a pest deterrent.

I am told, for instance, that if they are sprinkled on cabbages they will discourage cabbage worms. A fine sprinkling of wood ashes can also be put into the compost pile, once every 18 inches or so, and then covered with more organic matter.

Wood ashes lose a lot of their value if exposed to a soaking rain because the

potash leaches out of them easily. For this reason, it's a good idea to have *several* layers of ashes. Burning the skins of certain fruits and vegetables is a common practice among some purely organic gardeners. Ashes from banana skins, lemon skins, cucumbers, and cocoa shells have a very high phosphorus and potassium content.

Feathers

Pluckings from chickens, turkeys, and other fowl should be saved and composted. Feathers contain a large amount of nitrogen.

Garbage

Almost all organic kitchen refuse is excellent compost material. There are some notable exceptions: grease, oil, and animal fat — commonly known these days as *cholesterol*. The compost pile seems to have as much trouble breaking down fat as the human body does. For instance, bacon fat, thrown onto the pile when it is still liquid, can coat the fibers of some materials and preserve them almost as if they were varnished.

Meat scraps tend to attract animals and flies. If you can't bury them deep in your pile, it's best to avoid them. Also, avoid throwing dishwater into the pile, as it usually contains animal fats and grease.

Keep in mind that some communities have ordinances that restrict the type of waste that can be composted outdoors. For instance, in Seattle, Washington, food waste can only be composted outdoors if you (1) bury it under 1 foot of soil, or (2) use redworms in a worm composter to decompose it, or (3) use a tumbler that is on a stand above the ground. Restrictions such as these guard against odors that draw animals (especially rats) and flies. Take care that you're not attracting unseemly creatures to your compost pile.

Grass Clippings

People used to think that clippings contributed to thatch buildup in lawns and would take great pains to collect the clippings, bag them up, and set them aside to be disposed of. What a waste of nutrient-rich organic matter! Today, we know it's better to leave the clippings on the lawn, which is called "grasscycling," and if we're going to collect them it ought to be for the compost pile, not the landfill.

A word of caution before you dump bags of clippings on top of your pile: (1) Dry them first so they won't turn soggy and smelly, or (2) mix them with other dry, absorbent material (such as dead leaves) while they are still green (green clippings will help the pile heat up quickly), or (3) put them into your layer-cake pile in very thin layers.

There is some debate about whether it is safe to eat food grown in compost containing grass that has been sprayed with herbicides or pesticides. Some people contend that the chemicals break down during the composting process; others advise waiting a year after last using any chemical before saving your grass clippings for the compost pile. There is agreement that the longer you let the compost sit and cure after it's finished decomposing, the better. So, hot composting followed by a couple of months of curing will likely take care of any chemical residue. Better yet, avoid the toxic chemicals in the first place!

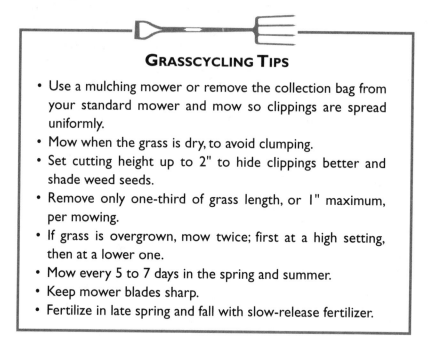

GRASSCYCLING TIPS

- Use a mulching mower or remove the collection bag from your standard mower and mow so clippings are spread uniformly.
- Mow when the grass is dry, to avoid clumping.
- Set cutting height up to 2" to hide clippings better and shade weed seeds.
- Remove only one-third of grass length, or 1" maximum, per mowing.
- If grass is overgrown, mow twice; first at a high setting, then at a lower one.
- Mow every 5 to 7 days in the spring and summer.
- Keep mower blades sharp.
- Fertilize in late spring and fall with slow-release fertilizer.

Ground Stone and Shells

Rocks and shells, of course, contain many minerals needed by plants. But it is awfully hard to dissolve a large stone, especially in plain water. Vermont is fortunate to have many quarries, making it easy for us to get stone dust. Granite or marble dust that has been pulverized into *very fine* particles will dissolve fairly quickly in any moist compost pile. By the time the compost is complete, many of these minerals are ready to be assimilated by plants. Ground oyster, clam, and lobster shells, to name just a few, will do the same thing. Pulverized oyster shells, by the way, make a fine lime substitute.

Hay or Straw

Dried hay or straw should be weathered first if it is going to make up a large percentage of the pile. The most compostable types of hay are those that have been left in a field, have turned gray, and are "spoiled," which only means that the hay is unfit for livestock feed. In many cases, a farmer is happy to get rid of this stuff at very little cost to you.

Unweathered straw or hay requires a tremendous amount of nitrogen if it is going to decay. In their efforts to break it down, bacteria may use up all of the existing nitrogen in a compost pile and still have enough to do a thorough job. If you find the explanation of the carbon to nitrogen ratio (see pages 38–40) too complicated to understand, or if you foresee some difficulty in making the proper adjustments in that ratio, it might be wise to use unweathered hay and straw in only very small amounts.

Hedge Trimmings

Hedge trimmings and branches pruned from trees are usually coarse and difficult to break down unless they are chopped or shredded, but an occasional layer of unchopped hedge trimmings can be used in the pile. They make good roughage and will permit air penetration. Don't overdo it, though, or your finished compost may be full of little undecomposed twigs.

Hops

Spent hops (brewery waste) make rich compost, even though they may have a beery smell for a while. A word of caution about hops: They are apt to be quite wet when you get them and will retain much of this moisture. A pile with a lot of spent hops will not need to be watered very often.

Keep checking to see that your pile is not overly moist. A pile that becomes too wet, of course, needs to be turned.

Leaves

Native Vermonters are sometimes amused by the "leaf freaks" who invade our state each autumn to enjoy the brilliant foliage. As a composter, you should become a "leaf freak" too. But learn to appreciate leaves for their nutritive as well as their aesthetic qualities. Deep tree roots do a fine job of retrieving trace elements from deep in the subsoil; the roots then give these minerals back to the leaves for temporary storage. Harvest leaves! Throwing them away is one of the worst kinds of conspicuous waste I know.

To be perfectly honest, leaves will break down quite slowly. A pile of leaves with nothing added may sit for years before it will be completely decomposed. Yet they should be an important part of anybody's compost pile. The chemical makeup of partially rotted leaves — or *leaf mold,* as it is called — is perhaps the closest thing in nature to pure humus. If you chop leaves and mix them with other things, they will decompose about four times as fast as they would normally. Try mixing five parts leaves with one part manure. If you have to use whole leaves, build them into the pile in a fairly thin, fairly dry layer. Incidentally, oak or beech leaves, if used exclusively, will make a slightly acidic compost, good for rhododendrons and blueberries.

DID YOU KNOW?

Chopping leaves reduces matting and speeds decomposition. Spread the leaves on the ground and run your lawn mower back and forth over the pile. Commercial leaf shredders can help you handle those big leaf piles.

Leather Waste

If you can get it, leather dust is very high in nitrogen and phosphorus. This is plentiful and inexpensive in some places.

Newspapers

Newspapers are one thing most of us have in abundance, and you'd probably be more than happy to avoid tying them up and hauling them to your recycler, or (shame, shame) hauling them to your landfill, or your trash can, or your curb. Anyway, newspapers are worth keeping around to add to your compost pile.

There has been some controversy about whether newspapers are safe to compost. Of concern is the carbon black ink, which contains polycyclic aromatic hydrocarbons (PAHs). These are known carcinogens, and people have wondered if it is safe to eat food grown in compost made with newspaper. Although the jury is still out, most scientific research to date indicates that PAHs are rendered inert by the temperatures of a hot compost pile, the biological activity, and the acids in the soil. Most newspaper inks no longer contain heavy metals, and most colored newsprint now uses vegetable dyes, so as long as you don't intensively compost with newspaper you can use it as a carbon source. Since it's not rich in nutrients like most organic matter, you'll want to use it sparingly anyway. Unless, of course, other organic matter is hard to come by. Be sure to shred the newspaper as finely as possible or it will mat and be slow to decompose.

TOO MANY NEWSPAPERS?

Newspapers can reduce the toil of digging up sod for a new garden bed. In the fall, simply spread them thickly on top of the sod and keep them wet with a hose until they freeze, or cover them with manure. They will smother the grass, and the following spring you can till and plant.

Peat Moss

I have long felt that peat moss is an overrated and over-priced gardening material. Peat adds almost nothing to your pile in terms of nutrient value, and if it is allowed to get too concentrated in one part of the pile it can absorb all of the moisture there, leaving the rest of the pile high and dry. Mixed thoroughly with other stuff, on the other hand, it makes a marvelous texturizer and conditioner for the compost because it rots so much more slowly than nearly everything else. After all, if everything were to disintegrate at the same speed, all of the particles of organic matter would be the same size, and your compost would have a uniform but less desirable consistency.

Pine Needles

Pine needles, including red and white pine as well as cedar, break down fairly slowly in a compost pile. They should be considered a good compost texturizer but should rarely be considered a major ingredient. They, like peat moss, oak leaves, and beech leaves, tend to make the pile slightly more acidic, but this should not necessarily be thought of as a negative quality because the rest of the materials may neutralize whatever acid effect they have.

Sawdust

Sawdust should be worked into the pile in thin sprinklings. If it gets too concentrated it will break down *very* slowly, and if it is too powdery it may form an airtight seal to boot. The ideal way to compost sawdust is to sandwich it between layers of manure. Oddly enough, softwood sawdusts (pine, spruce, cedar, etc.) break down much more slowly than hardwood sawdusts (maple, oak, birch, etc.). Weathered sawdust decomposes much more readily than fresh.

Seaweed (Kelp)

Seaweed is a good source of potassium, and you can take advantage of its nutrient content when growing potassium-hungry crops like potatoes. It rots easily and can be mixed with something that has a lot of bulk, such as straw. Seaweed also contains boron, iodine, calcium, magnesium, sodium, and other trace elements. It may be easy to get too *many* "goodies," particularly sodium, from seaweed. If it is to be put directly on the garden in large amounts, this should be done only about once every three or four years. We haven't yet figured out exactly *what* percentage of an average compost pile should be composed of seaweed, but I have been assured that it is nothing to worry about so long as the majority of the pile is not kelp.

One gardener I know maintains that a thick blanket of seaweed is better than anything else — organic or artificial — for keeping a pile well insulated in wintertime. Seaweed in its granular form — kelp meal — can be sprinkled on your compost pile to get it cooking.

Sod

In one shot, sod should add both loam (good topsoil) *and* organic matter to your compost. But don't dig up turf from somewhere and throw it into the pile in one big clump. Distribute it throughout some of the material that is already there. Sod is a splendid insulator, and it should also keep flies away. Try covering the top of your pile with sod — roots up, grass down. If you do this in the fall, by spring the sod will have disappeared.

VEGETABLE PLANTS AND ANNUAL FLOWERS

After feeding your stomachs and your spirits all summer, these plants are ready to feed your soil. Add them to your compost pile or till them into your garden. To be on the safe side, burn any diseased plants.

Weeds

I stopped to see a friend not long ago, just as he had finished weeding his garden. He had all of the weeds neatly packed in boxes ready to be taken to the dump. Most of the weeds he had pulled had already gone to seed. Fearing that by tilling them directly back into the garden between his rows he would only be propagating the various weed species, he had elected to sacrifice the organic matter they contained in the hope of saving himself some work later on. I didn't tell him so, but I couldn't help thinking that with a good active compost pile he could have had his cake and eaten it, too.

He could have kept the organic matter and allowed the pile to "thermal kill" the weed seeds. Once exposed to the temperatures at which thermophilic bacteria operate, most weed seeds cannot survive for long. But there are other ways that weed seeds can be done in. I understand that a seed subjected to the digestive system of an earthworm can never germinate.

If you add weeds to your pile, remember: The more weed seeds you have, the greater the need for manure or some other nitrogen-rich material to *ensure* sufficient heating. The temperature should reach 135°F for a few days. Weeds that have gone to seed should be put near the center of the pile where the heat is most intense. If you just leave them on the surface of the pile, some seeds will germinate and begin to grow there.

Composting weeds can save you work in another way, too: There is no need to shake all of the dirt off the roots. Adding soil to the heap will *improve* the compost. In fact, soil is one of the best natural activators.

Stubborn Materials

Corncobs, apple pomace (even though it smells nice), citrus rinds, cotton stalks, sugarcane leaves (*not* bagasse, which is the cane residue), and palm fronds all are on the list of vegetable materials that are hardest to rot. To help them along, they should be mixed with stuff that will easily break down. If possible, they should be chopped, too.

Cornstalks and husks are nearly as opposed to being decayed as are the cobs. The best and safest way to deal with them — and prevent corn diseases — is to till them under the soil. If you are going to compost them, they *must* be run through a shredder. Apple pomace, like spent hops, contains lots of moisture and should be spread in thin layers. Also, the apple seeds in it seem to have a great resistance to heat. They may survive until after the pile is cooled.

Peanut hulls decompose quite easily and contribute lots of nitrogen. Walnut, pecan, and almond shells, on the other hand, break down very slowly. They, like stone, contain many important minerals. A good chopper can pulverize them enough so that they will rot in a fraction of the time it would normally take for them to decay. And some woody materials may take a couple of years to compost completely.

Thalassa Cruso, in *Making Things Grow Outdoors*, reminds us that prickly things like rose bushes and raspberry canes can produce a thorny problem. Thorns themselves, it seems, are so hard that they resist decomposition and are too small to be effectively chopped by a machine. The cane will rot fine, but the thorns might lie peacefully in the pile waiting for a chance to rise up and attack you as you are handling the compost later.

Materials to Avoid

You might be tempted someday, when your pile has shrunk and looks disappointingly small, to "beef up" the volume of your heap by adding soil other than good loam or humus. Mud, sand, and gravel add little to either the nutrient or the bacterial value of your compost. Following is a listing of some other things to avoid.

Coal, Charcoal

Most ashes are safe to mix into your compost heap, but coal ashes are not. They have *excessive* amounts of both sulfur and iron, amounts that are toxic to plants. Charcoal should be avoided, too. This is something that many of us have a lot of because we use charcoal briquettes for outdoor cooking. The temptation is to throw partially burned charcoal on the compost pile. I have tried it. Months later I found that it had not decayed at all. No wonder. Archaeologists have discovered on more than one occasion that charcoal, which is primarily carbon, will resist decay even after thousands of years.

Colored Paper

Most glossy paper, including magazines, catalogs, and colored newsprint, no longer contains heavy metals and can be added to your compost pile in small amounts. Because the paper is mostly cellulose, it will break down slowly and use up a good deal of nitrogen in the process. Shred the paper to speed decomposition and to keep it from forming an impenetrable layer in the pile.

Diseased Plants

I have stumbled on a leaflet put out by the Irish Department of Agriculture and Fisheries in Dublin that is called, simply enough, "Compost." The Irish, who should know about as much as anyone in the world when it comes to growing potatoes, are nervous about certain plant debris that could contain disease organisms that might have a chance of surviving the "thermal kill" of the composting process. They warn that potato tubers affected by wart disease and potato stalks invaded by *sclerotia* (dark, flat bodies that indicate stalk disease) should not be thrown into the pile.

They also tell us to beware specifically of cabbage that has been affected by club root, root crops suffering from dry rot, celery leaves affected by leaf spot or blight, and onions that have been attacked by onion mildew. It takes an ideal compost system to provide the conditions necessary to destroy the pathogenic organisms that cause these diseases. Any vegetable matter that is questionable should be burned, especially if you are doubtful about your pile's ability to heat sufficiently. Then, and only then, the ashes should be perfectly safe, and can be added to the pile.

FOODS TO AVOID

- Meat
- Fish
- Grease, oil, fat

Nonbiodegradable Items

It used to be that you could compost nearly any kind of old fabric or rags. Today, an organic garment seems more the exception than the rule — most clothes now include synthetic materials. These are all nonbiodegradable. I am sure I don't need to remind you to keep all nonbiodegradable substances, including plastic, glass, and aluminum objects, out of your compost heap. It is not that they will do any particular harm there, but they will never do any good. Real rubber is organic in origin but slow to rot. Don't try to compost it.

Pet Litter

You may have already heard that pregnant women and children shouldn't handle cat litter. This is because cat droppings may contain dangerous organisms that can cause blindness, especially in children. *Toxoplasma gondii* is a parasite that can be transmitted to the fetus,

causing brain and eye disease. *Toxocra cati* is a nematode that can enter the blood stream by mouth and cause infection of the eyes and other organs. For these same reasons, keep cat droppings and litter out of your compost pile. Dog droppings also may contain disease organisms and are best avoided.

Sludge

Sludge needs special handling and high temperatures to kill disease organisms and get rid of toxic metals. For these reasons, don't try to compost your own waste. If you live in a small town with no industry, the sludge from your sewage treatment facility may be safe enough to use since toxic metals probably won't be the problem they are in larger cities. But to be on the safe side, the compost experts I've talked to don't recommend using sludge. There is one exception: the commercially available treated sludge that's sold in bags at garden centers. These products normally come under close Environmental Protection Agency (EPA) scrutiny and are considered safe for home gardeners.

Toxic Chemicals

I have heard that some people put insecticides, pesticides, or poisons in their piles to keep insects and annoying animals out. This is harmful! Adding such things to your pile kills off the beneficial microorganisms that are creating your compost. Such poisons have no place in the natural microcommunity of your compost pile.

Carbon-to-Nitrogen Ratio

As you gather materials, there's one more thing to keep in mind: the ratio of the carbon (C) materials to nitrogen (N) matter in your compost system. Scientists have determined

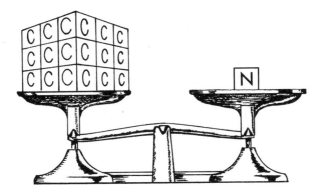

that a good ratio of carbon to nitrogen in a compost pile is about 25 to 30 parts carbon to 1 part nitrogen, or 30:1 (commonly shortened to "30"). In practical terms, this means most of the materials you add should be carbon materials. A pile with a C/N much higher than 25 to 30 will take a long time to decompose. This is why a pile of oak leaves or a mound of sawdust and wood chips will sit for years without much apparent decay. If the C/N ratio is very low (that is, if there is too much nitrogen), your pile will likely release the excess as smelly ammonia gas.

Here are the average C/Ns for some compostable materials that are often used:

Compostable Material	Average C/N
Alder or ash leaves	25
Grass clippings	25
Leguminous plants (peas, beans, soybeans)	15
Manure with bedding	23
Manure	15
Oak leaves	50
Pine needles	60–100
Sawdust	150–500
Straw, cornstalks and cobs	50–100
Vegetable trimmings	25

But the C/N ratio need not be exact. You will have no precise way of measuring it, anyway. In general, add 2 to 3 pounds of nitrogen materials for every 100 pounds of carbon materials. If you use lots of sawdust, which is very high in carbon, you may need to add even more nitrogen than that.

I prefer to put up with a slight odor and keep a small surplus of nitrogen in the pile, just to make sure there is always enough to speed decomposition.

Activators Get Things Cooking!

Don't forget that, given enough time, any biodegradable material will eventually rot. We have learned something about some of the things that could go into a composting system to make up the bulk of the final product. Now we need to think about some sort of activator, a catalyst or "starter" that will get things going microbiologically, an accelerator that can expedite the natural decomposition process. Activators are more than special ingredients that add "sugar and spice" to the compost. They are vital elements — simple as they may be — in the potluck recipe you are concocting. Trying to make good compost without an activator is like trying to make concrete without cement.

One of history's earliest records having to do with gardening tells us that the ancient Babylonians used the blood from camels and other creatures (one source tells us that they preferred *human* blood) as a compost activator. Barbaric as this may seem to the squeamish twentieth-century mind, it should be noted that a great many successful composters use dried blood or blood meal — which is collected at slaughterhouses, dried, and packaged — as a compost activator today. I have used it myself. As long as it is dry, it is nearly odorless and quite clean. It is no more than a very dark red, almost black, powdery substance. I have no qualms at all about picking it out of the bag with my bare hands and throwing it on the pile.

This is not to suggest that you should worry about getting *your* hands on anything as exotic or expensive as blood meal to use as an activator for your compost. If you *do* use it, it can be put to even better use as a fertilizer or pest repellent. Sprinkle some around the edges of your garden space or right in the rows among young beans and peas. Woodchucks and rabbits, who love nibbling on such tender young things, seem to be frightened by its scent. Dogs, unfortunately, think it smells great, and will do their best to lick it up.

Remember: By adding an activator to your compost heap all you are trying to do is to provide a nitrogen-protein source that will feed the microcommunity. Once the microcommunity begins working and reproducing, your compost pile will be functioning near its top efficiency.

Finished compost and soil are also considered activators because they provide microorganisms and enzymes. Commercial products that contain dormant bacteria and fungi are another kind of activator. Let's take a look at all of these.

Compost

One of the best activators is what is sometimes called "seeding compost." This is no more than "ripe" or finished compost that is left over or borrowed from another pile. A little of this will supply the new material

NATURAL ACTIVATORS

Alfalfa meal
Blood meal
Bone meal
Compost
Cottonseed meal
Fish meal
Hoof meal
Horn meal
Manure
Soil

with all kinds of microorganisms and possibly even a few earthworms, which can become the founding fathers of a new colony. A 2-inch layer of seeding compost can be put into your pile on top of every 12 inches or so of new organic matter.

Some people like to douse their heaps with strong compost or rich soil "tea." This can be brewed simply by filling a burlap or cheesecloth bag with good earth or compost and letting it sit in a bucket or barrel of water for several days. The resulting dark liquid is a good compost activator and an even better side-dressing for droopy plants that seem to need a quick boost. (See page 137 for an example of this contraption.)

Manure

Manure is a rich source of both nitrogen and beneficial bacteria, making it one of the most valuable additions to your compost pile. It also contains phosphorus and potassium, which are essential plant nutrients.

Some of the more common manures used are bat (guano), cow, duck, goat, goose, hen, horse, pig, pigeon, rabbit, sheep, and turkey manures. Fresh manure may contain as much as 80 percent water; it should be allowed to dry out a bit so it will not affect the water content of the pile or cut off the free passage of air to and from the different layers in the heap.

Horse, sheep, and poultry manures are sometimes called "hot manures." If they are used when they are too fresh, they can stimulate such frenzied bacterial activity that many of the pile's beneficial microorganisms are killed along with the harmful ones. Hot manures quickly inspire the generation of enough intense heat to kill earthworms and other macroorganisms.

Poultry manure seems to be one of the most potent activators. Newspaper, one of those stubborn materials mentioned in the last chapter, will decompose much more quickly if chicken, goose, or duck manure is added to it. Poultry manure should be diluted and weakened by the addition of litter, which usually consists of sawdust, shavings, or chopped straw.

Well-rotted manure is the safest kind to use in the compost heap. It is usually lighter in color than fresh manure, drier, and not nearly as smelly. There are literally tons of rotted manure in rural areas, particularly in the spring after farmers have been emptying out their barns all winter. They will usually sell it cheap if you are willing to load it and cart it home yourself. If you have farm animals of your own, collect their droppings and leave them exposed to the weather for a few weeks before using them in the compost heap.

One concern about using manure is the presence of weed seeds that grazing animals pass on. If your pile reaches high enough temperatures, weed seeds should be killed off; however, if you find that you are having a problem with weeds after applying compost, manure may be the cause.

Meal

Vegetarians generally prefer not to use animal products in their compost. An excellent substitute is any kind of protein meal such as that from alfalfa or cottonseed. They are somewhat expensive, but less so than blood meal, fish meal, hoof meal, or horn meal. They have a pleasant smell, are easy to handle, and are not hard to find in many areas of the country. The downside of cottonseed meal is that it may contain pesticide residue from sprays applied to cotton fields. Generally, it's not considered an organic fertilizer.

It's the simplest thing in the world to activate your pile with protein meal. Just add a heavy sprinkling every 6 inches or so, add water, and within 48 hours your heap will be warm in the center.

An associate of ours was invited to a neighboring town not too long ago to give a short talk on vegetable gardening and composting. He loaded all sorts of gardening tools and paraphernalia into the back of a pickup truck and took off for Lyndonville, Vermont. When he arrived he discovered that he had forgotten to bring along anything to activate the demonstration compost pile he had planned to build. Rather than panic, he went to the nearest grocery store, bought a 50-pound bag of dry dog food, returned, and later sprinkled layers of it into the pile. Most dog foods contain meal — except the ones whose manufacturers insist otherwise, of course — and are quite naturally packed with protein. A pretty expensive compost was made in Lyndonville that day, but some of the local people say that it was just great when it was finished.

Soil

Soil itself is teeming with microbial life. The best kind of soil to use as an activator is what you and I know as loam. *Loam* is a mixture of sand, silt, clay, and decaying organic matter. You can use it in layers about 2 inches thick — one layer of soil for every 6 inches or so of other matter.

It is probably a good idea not to take soil from a field or orchard where poisonous herbicide sprays and insecticides have been used. Such things, as you already know, remain in the soil for some time and can be toxic to the bacteria. Soil from the woods might be all right. It might also prove to be quite acidic, but lime will cure that. *Muck* — that black soil dug out of swampy areas — is also good for activating a pile.

Artificial Activators

There are certain chemicals — if you are into using such things — that can bring up the nitrogen level of the compost pile. Purists call this "spiking" and look upon it with disfavor. But it may be the best solution for you.

You might use a "complete" fertilizer such as 10-5-10. A typical composting formula would be to use 1 cup of fertilizer for every 10 square feet of level pile surface. This could be applied again each time your pile rose by 6 inches. You could also use calcium nitrate or sodium nitrate in slightly lesser amounts. These will tend to leave a faintly acidic residue in the pile, but this "sourness" can be easily neutralized by adding some alkaline material like lime (see chapter 10 on pH). There is some evidence that ammonium sulfate is toxic to earthworms, so to be on the safe side, avoid using it.

Some gardeners add fertilizers such as superphosphate or muriate of potash to their compost-in-the-making. A few of those I have talked to are slightly confused, thinking that such things will help to activate the dormant bacteria and fungi that are already in the pile. Unfortunately, that doesn't work. However, they may be helping to produce a more perfectly balanced compost because the phosphorus and potassium might remain held in the compost for later use by garden plants.

In general, though, chemical fertilizer is not particularly effective as an activator because unlike animal matter and some vegetable matter, it contains no protein. In fact, chemicals will probably be more valuable if applied to compost after it is finished (the "goodies" are less likely to be leached out that way) or to the garden soil directly.

Bacterial Activators

Bacterial activators — or inoculants, as they are sometimes called — usually consist of granules or tablets made up of a substance that includes dormant bacteria and fungi. The theory behind using them is that they introduce the proper microorganisms into the pile and assure a rapid and satisfactory decomposition.

I have tried the bacterial activator that comes in the form of effervescent tablets, each of which is meant to be dissolved in a gallon of water. The tablets look and act something like Alka-Seltzer. I kept a gallon of water-activator mixture around the house and each day would put some of it in the old kitchen blender that I use to grind up kitchen refuse before I threw it on the compost pile. Every time a quart or so of garbage was ground up, millions of the right bacteria should have been added and thoroughly distributed throughout the material. Once on the pile, it was hard for my unscientific eye to see that this stuff was rotting any faster than other

garbage that had passed through the blender and was mixed with plain water.

Granted, I'm a pretty conscientious composter, and I add soil and finished compost to new batches-in-the-works, so I'm probably adding the right microorganisms at the same time. If you don't have soil or compost to activate your pile, a bacterial activator might be a good insurance policy. There is some evidence that these activators can increase the speed of decomposition with less loss of ammonia and less leaching of nutrients. They also can be helpful if you live in areas of low rainfall, high heat, or extreme cold, where there is less bacterial survival. You might want to conduct your own experiment with activators and see if they make a difference. At the very least, they do no harm.

Composting will be a whole lot simpler for you if you acknowledge the fact that the right bacteria, fungi, and actinomycetes already exist within your compost pile. The potential for excellent decomposition is right there. Let Mother Nature worry about adjusting the various populations within the microcommunity. That's her job, and she does it well.

Composting Methods to Stimulate Your Imagination

Now that some groundwork has been laid, in the form of a few composting fundamentals, let's have a look at some well-publicized recipes and methods. But don't try to use any one of these descriptions as a definitive model. A smart composter, like a good cook or experienced carpenter, adapts recipes or blueprints to fit his or her needs and materials. There is no known law that says you cannot be composting several different ways at the same time.

Heaps

Heaps require the least amount of work to get started. Simply pile up your materials in an open area, preferably the future site of a garden so any nutrients leached from the pile will be put to use eventually. A good size to aim for is 5 feet wide, 3 feet high, and as long as it needs to be. The best idea is to make at least two piles. When the first pile is big enough, make another. That way, you can have piles at different stages of decomposition going at the same time. Following are some variations on this theme.

The Indore Process

In a book called *Soil and Health: A Study of Organic Agriculture*, published in 1947, England's Sir Albert Howard defined the composting process in fairly concise terms:

> *[It is] the collection and admixture of vegetable and animal wastes off of the area farmed into heaps or pits, kept at a degree of moisture resembling that of a squeezed-out sponge, turned, and emerging at the end of three months as a rich, crumbling compost, containing a wealth of plant nutrients and organics essential for growth.*

Sir Albert was concerned about what he called the "waste products of agriculture," which he saw as too valuable to simply throw away. In this sense, by making a real effort to find something truly beneficial to do with them, he was a man far ahead of his time, a forerunner of the organic-conservationist-ecology movement that was still waiting in the wings.

A reading of Sir Albert's complex descriptions of his Indore composting procedures would impress you with the exactitude of his scientific investigations. You might also get the distinct impression, I am sorry to say, that if you did not follow his instructions to the letter, nothing in the way of decomposition would happen in your compost pile.

This, as you have been assured many times before, is nonsense. Rotting is rotting. Working microorganisms haven't the slightest notion whether they exist in some scientifically conceived compost system or whether they are in a lonely and forgotten corner of someone's woodlot.

Today, several generations after his original writings were published, it is easy to belittle and criticize Sir Albert's work. Let us not forget, however, that his efforts were those of a pioneer in what was, for most of Western civilization, at least, a nearly forgotten field. Let's remember, too, that his extremely specific and precise directions for making compost were especially suited for a particular set of physical and climatic conditions in Indore, India, where the early experiments were performed.

Despite his apparent inflexibility, Sir Albert's composting methods were based on four valid principles, all of which are still applicable:

1. The building of compost piles in *sandwich-like layers* to encourage the alternation of green or wet materials with dry, withered matter.
2. The necessity of *accurate moisture content* within the pile, in order for the microbial life to operate efficiently.
3. *Optimum pile size,* taking into consideration the problems of compaction, heating, and insulation.
4. Ultimately *good aeration,* which allows the growth of aerobic bacteria as one of the requirements for good decomposition.

In the actual Indore process, Sir Albert was composting on a much larger scale than he later recommended for the New Zealand box, which he saw as a convenient-sized container for the home gardener. His original piles and pits, which were anaerobic in most cases, held a much greater volume of materials than the New Zealand box would have. He recommended an "admixture" of wastes that consisted of two-thirds vegetable matter, one-third manure, and an amount of activator equal to 1 percent of the vegetable waste.

For those of us like you and me who already know a *little* bit about compost science, there is nothing new here really. Since the 1940s, gardening specialists have improved upon some of these techniques and expanded some of Sir Albert's principles. We can thank him directly for much of what we now know about modern composting.

HOW TO CONSTRUCT AN INDORE PILE

1. Lay down alternate 6-inch layers of green and dry vegetable matter, 2 inches of manure on top of that, and then a sprinkling of dried blood, hoof and horn meal, or soil.

2. Complete the same layering process again.

3. Water the heap until it has the consistency of a squeezed-out sponge.

4. Poke ventilation holes in the pile with a long crowbar. These holes should reach right down to the earth at the bottom of the pile.

5. For the first six weeks after the pile has been started, the composter should heed two danger signals:

   a. A bad odor with the presence of flies, meaning that the pile has been overwatered

   b. "Arrested fermentation" caused by too little watering.

6. After the first six weeks, remove the material from the original pile and build a second one with it, turning and remixing the organic matter as you do so. This time there is no need to worry about layering.

7. Allow the compost in the second pile to ripen as you begin making a new pile out of fresh materials on the site of the first one.

8. By the end of another six weeks (about three months all told), the batch of compost in the second pile should be "finished" and ready for use.

AN ALTERNATIVE COMPOSTING SYSTEM

Much like a mini-trench silo, this system is modeled after the open concrete areas used for storing silage on large livestock farms.

This is a good way to get around having to turn your compost by hand, and a great way to put your rotary tiller to good use at times when you are not able to use it in the garden.

The distance between the plywood sidewalls should be just a little greater than the width of the tiller. Pile organic matter in the open-ended container, making the pile highest in the center and tapering it gradually toward either end. As you drive your machine through, the tines should mix and turn the material for you.

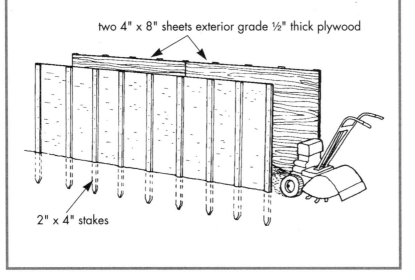

two 4" x 8" sheets exterior grade ½" thick plywood

2" x 4" stakes

┌───┐
│   │
│   │
│ **UNIVERSITY OF CALIFORNIA METHOD ESSENTIALS** │
│   │
│ 1. *Chopping or shredding* to increase the surface area of the organic materials. │
│   │
│ 2. A *thorough blending* of a nitrogenous activator like manure, and carbonaceous materials such as leaves and grass clippings. │
│   │
│ 3. *Frequent turning,* every three days at least, to improve aeration and expose all materials to heat in the center of the pile. │
│   │
└───┘

The University of California Method

If you are just starting a garden and feel you need compost "right now," I would say that the University of California method is more than worth the effort. With it you can make usable compost in fourteen days.

One Saturday morning last October, I started a new compost pile by following, more or less, the principles of the University of California method. The pile was to consist of leaves of all kinds, already rotting sticks from the woods surrounding my house, and seedy first-cut hay, which I brought home in bales.

Everything was chopped before it went into the heap and was pretty thoroughly mixed. First, a big handful of hay was fed into the shredder, then a handful of leaves, a handful of dead sticks, and so on. The pile measured about 5 feet by 4 feet. Whenever it built up 3 or 4 inches, it was given a generous sprinkling of alfalfa meal and was heavily dampened with water from the garden hose. Every 18 inches or so, a thick layer of coarse, unchopped hay was added, just to provide clear air channels into the pile.

By midafternoon the pile was about 5 feet high. I closed off the open side of the wire-fence compost enclosure by stacking several extra bales of hay there. Then I broke one or two more bales so that I could put a thick layer of tightly packed "books" or "flakes" of hay on top of the pile for insulation. I then wet down the whole pile one more time for good measure.

By Sunday morning, the compost pile was already warm. In less than a day, the bacteria already in the compost material had decided among themselves who was going to take over and do most of the initial work. They had become so enthusiastic about their project that they were already producing a lot of heat. By Sunday night, the pile exuded steamy vapor. On Monday morning there was a heavy frost, but it was clear to me that the heap had already shrunk. The temperature was too high for me to comfortably put my hand beneath the top layers of hay.

Tuesday evening the pile was turned for the first time. And it was turned again every three days after that. On the third Saturday, exactly two weeks after it was made, the pile had cooled down. It was torn apart, loaded into the garden cart, hauled away to the garden in several trips, and spread there. It was certainly a far cry from the dark "crumbling compost" that Sir Albert Howard described, but it had obviously been through partial sterilization as a result of the heat. It was riddled with actinomycetes, the weed seeds had apparently been killed (at least few of them germinated in the spring), and despite the stringiness caused by the unchopped hay, it smelled rich, earthy, and fertile.

By late spring its final decomposition in the garden proper was complete. The soil revealed no evidence of any of the particles of organic matter in the compost, including the wood chips from the old sticks — even though the garden had been through a cold winter with very little snow-cover protection. Not a bad testimonial for the University of California method, I would say.

The Ogden Three-Pile System

If professors at the University of California tell the short of it, Samuel Ogden, a Vermont author and organic gardening guru, was their antithesis. He took the long route — nearly two years of decomposition to complete his compost.

He introduced his method in his book *Step-by-Step to Organic Vegetable Gardening*. Using three piles, each measuring 5 feet by 12 feet within cinder block or sod-retaining walls, every year Ogden removed finished compost from one and built another, while the third pile just sat there rotting, undisturbed. Throughout the summer, he added garden residues to the pile, along with topsoil, and once in a while an application of manure. In the fall, Ogden covered the pile with overturned sod or manure.

He kept leaves and fresh grass clippings out of his pile, believing that leaves were too tough and grass clippings turned slimy. I think it's a shame not to take advantage of all those leaves we are blessed (or cursed) with in the fall. They provide carbon as well as add bulk to the pile, which helps aeration. So I recommend either shredding the leaves or thoroughly mixing them with other compost materials. Also, if your pile is fast-acting (as opposed to Ogden's slow, anaerobic pile), raw grass clippings won't turn smelly and slimy. They are an excellent source of nitrogen — too good to waste.

Ogden described his composting style as "the lazy man's method." He did no turning and allowed rainfall to take care of all his watering chores. He used his compost pile to recycle his garden debris and to create the next best thing to stable manure. This is how he described the process:

> The difference between manure and compost is simple: in the first instance an animal feeds on vegetation and passes the material through the body, extracting nourishment in the process. Thus the waste consists of organic material that has been fragmented and treated with body juice, then subjected to further

decomposition due to the complicated action of oxygen and bacteria while the manure is stacked in piles. Compost is, in general, made the same way, with the exception that one step in the process is omitted, that of passing through the body of some animal. The end products are highly similar and, for our purposes, nearly identical. . . . A compost pile is a sensible and even necessary adjunct to a garden, for it means the conservation of waste and a reduction in the expense of operation.

The Biodynamic Compost Pile

The Biodynamic Farming and Gardening Method is a kind of practical philosophy of farming and gardening. It was developed from the teachings of Rudolf Steiner, a philosopher known for his world view called *anthroposophy*, which emphasizes the unity of all life processes. Biodynamic principles are similar to organic gardening tenets, but they go a step further by including exacting steps to producing humus. The organic material to be used as a basis for compost is transformed either by particular biodynamic preparations or by a biodynamic compost starter.

The preparations are made from plants that have traditionally been used as medicinal herbs. The plants themselves are prepared according to specific recipes. These biodynamic preparations are believed to transform the organic material and produce superior compost. Proponents believe the fertilizer value of manure and compost can be considerably increased by their method.

Ehrenfried Pfeiffer, who was a director of the Biochemical Research Laboratory at the Goetheanum Dornach, Switzerland, and a follower of Steiner's, did much to spread the word about biodynamic farming and gardening through his writings. He also devised the formula for the compost starter.

The biodynamic compost pile should be built with a maximum width at the bottom of 12 feet and a minimum height of

2 to 3 feet (a maximum of 5 feet), with slanting sides. The pile can be as long as desired. Materials are spread in layers not more than 2 inches thick, and each layer is sprinkled with soil and with the Biodynamic Compost Starter solution. The pile is covered with a layer of straw, hay, leaves, etc. If the materials are mixed beforehand, the compost starter solution should be sprayed into the mixture.

If you'd like to know more about the biodynamic method, contact the Biodynamic Association, Inc. (see Sources for address).

A Quick Leaf Compost

One fast method calls for laying out leaves on the ground and adding fresh manure and a little compost or soil. Rototill them all together and add water, if needed. Then pile the materials at least 3 feet high, 6 feet wide, and however long you wish. Cover with plastic for four or five days. Then remove the plastic and rototill again to aerate, and build the pile again, replacing the cover. In another two weeks, your compost will be ready to use.

Sheet-Composting

Sheet-composting and using green manures (see page 61) are the primary alternatives to a compost pile for getting vast amounts of organic matter into your garden's soil. They are certainly more direct because, in a sense, you're eliminating the middle man, the compost pile itself. No nutrients can be lost through leaching as they inevitably must be to a certain extent from a compost heap. At the same time, there is no possibility of thermal kill and no way that weed seeds can be killed *en masse* without using strong chemicals.

Sheet-composting is sometimes confused with mulching. When you mulch with organic matter you are slowly feeding the soil, but your main interest is in reducing weeds and evaporation of moisture from the soil by laying something on the surface of the ground. Sheet-composting involves mixing organic materials with the soil itself, usually with the help of a spade or rototiller. It's an ideal way to improve soils that contain too much clay, gravel, or builder's fill. It will also help to protect garden spots threatened by erosion.

Leaves, grass clippings, manure — whatever organic matter you can gather will work. Leaves, as you know, abound in trace elements. Green grass clippings contain nitrogen and need not be dried before being tilled under. Almost any kind of healthy organic matter, in fact, will provide nourishment for the microorganisms and earthworms in the garden.

Sheet-composting is done at the end of the gardening season because the materials need several months to break down in the soil. One drawback of this method is that if you add mostly carbon materials, they will draw upon the nitrogen already present in the soil to aid in decomposition. Even if you use grass clippings, they may release their nitrogen too quickly. For this reason, it's a good idea to also add some nitrogen materials such as manure, blood meal, or cottonseed meal. You might also add natural rock powders such as rock phosphate (for phosphorus) and granite dust (for potassium).

To use a rototiller to mix these materials into the soil, you simply spread them on top of the soil, set the machine to maximum tilling depth, and till everything under.

A Creative Collection Method

Last fall, a neighbor-friend borrowed my pickup truck and my two children for an afternoon. He has a tiny garden plot (it can't be more than 12 by 40 feet), but his careful management allows him to grow a surprising abundance of vegetables. He lives on a ledge and had to bring in topsoil in order to have a garden at all.

Together with my two children and two children of his own, he drove slowly around the nearby countryside loading all the leaves he could find and easily rake up into the back of the truck. Each time he loaded up with more leaves, he asked the kids to jump and play in them. Naturally, they were delighted to oblige. When the leaves got pretty well packed down, he told them to sit down in the back of the truck while he drove to find more. He harvested three truckloads this way, which with the fine compaction he used must have amounted to a dozen or more loads.

Later that quiet Sunday afternoon, I began to wonder what had become of the children. I wandered down the road until I heard screams of delight coming from behind my neighbor's house. When I got closer, I could see the four young ones still romping and wrestling in the leaves, which by this time lay a foot and a half or two feet thick on top of the garden.

My friend was just coming around the corner of the barn with the rear-end tiller. I really doubted that he would be able to till all those leaves into the garden. But, sure enough, after three or four passes with the machine, most of them were buried — much to the disgust of four very dirty youngsters. This spring every remnant of the leaves has disappeared, and my friend's little garden seems to have at least 2 or 3 more inches of soil than it had last year.

GREEN MANURES

Green manures are not those that have come fresh from the cow or horse. They are cover crops like buckwheat or rye. Using green manures is like sheet-composting with living green matter that grows right in place. Crop residues such as cornstalks, tomato vines, pea plants, or thick-rooted crops like kale can also be tilled under as green manures.

Growing cover crops for the express purpose of turning them under is best done either in the off-growing season (ryegrass will show good growth in the fall and early spring) or in some portion of the garden that is left fallow. Roots of green manure crops will grow deep into the subsoil, retrieving nutrients that have leached beyond the reach of many vegetable plants' roots.

Cover-cropping is an excellent way to rejuvenate overworked soil, or to prepare a new area for a vegetable or flower garden. A cover crop should be tilled under at least six weeks before the next crop is planted. You can plant a cover crop in early fall, till it under in late fall, and plant another cover crop to overwinter and begin growth in early spring. Then you can till it under six weeks before planting your spring garden.

Just as with sheet-composting, the vegetation will likely take nitrogen from the soil as it decomposes, even though it will eventually release more nitrogen than it uses up. That's the reason for waiting at least six weeks after tilling manure crops before planting your garden. Legumes like peas, beans, soybeans, cowpeas, alfalfa, clover, and vetch are especially valuable because they attract nitrogen-fixing bacteria to their roots and contribute lots of nitrogen to the soil. Other green manures like buckwheat, annual and perennial ryegrass, oats, wheat, sorghum and, yes, common weeds, will add good organic material to your garden. Try it. Refer to the chart on pages 62–63 for some general planting guidelines. For more information, consult Storey Publishing bulletin A-5 Cover Crop Gardening.

Spring and Summer Seeding	Seeding Rate (lbs./acre)	Seeding Rate (lbs./1000 sq.ft.)	Depth to Cover Seed (in.)	Adapted to Soils of Low Fertility
LEGUMES				
Alfalfa	20	1	½	N
Beans, Snap	—	15	1½	Y
Beans, Soy	90	5	1½	Y
Clover, Alsike	10	½	½	N
Clover, Red	10	½	½	N
Clover, White	10	½	½	N
Cowpeas	90	5	1½	Y
Sweet Clover, White	15	½	½	Y
Sweet Clover, Yellow	15	½	½	Y
NONLEGUMES				
Buckwheat	75	2	¾	Y
Sudan Grass	35	1	¾	N

Late Summer and Fall Seeding

	Seeding Rate (lbs./acre)	Seeding Rate (lbs./1000 sq.ft.)	Depth to Cover Seed (in.)	Adapted to Soils of Low Fertility
LEGUMES				
Clover, Crimson	30	1	½	N
Lupine, Blue	100	2½	1	N
Lupine, White	150	4	1	N
Lupine, Yellow	80	2	1	Y
Pea, Field	90	5	1½	Y
Sweet Clover, Yellow Annual (Sourclover)	15	½	½	Y
Vetch, Common	60	2	¾	N
Vetch, Hairy	40	1½	¾	N
Vetch, Hungarian	60	2	¾	N
Vetch, Purple	60	2	¾	N
NONLEGUMES				
Barley	100	2½	¾	N
Kale	15	½	½	N
Oats	100	2½	1	N
Rye	100	2½	¾	Y
Ryegrass, Annual	35	1	¾	Y
Wheat	100	2½	¾	N

Areas of U.S. Where Best Adapted	Comments
All	Has deep roots and is excellent for mulch. Needs a pH of 6 or higher. Should grow a full season.
All	Broadcast in wide rows. Harvest before turning under.
All	Can be turned under early or be allowed to mature and harvested.
North	Good for areas too wet or acid for red clover.
North & Central	Needs a pH of 6 or higher. Should grow a full season. Can be cut for mulch.
All	Needs a pH of 6 or higher. The giant variety, Ladino, is best for green manure.
South & Central	Fast-growing crop for hot, dry weather. Drought resistant.
All	Needs a pH of 6 to 7. Should grow a full season. Has strong, deep taproot.
All	Similar to white variety but does better under dry conditions.
All	Fast-growing warm-season crop. Grows in most any soil and can smother weeds.
All	Makes rapid, vigorous growth during the hottest part of the summer.
South & Central	One of the best winter annuals from New Jersey southward.
Gulf Coast	Most widely used of the lupines. Needs moderate fertility.
Deep South	The most winter-hardy lupine. Needs neutral, fairly fertile soil.
Florida	Least winter-hardy of lupines. Does well in moderately acid, infertile soil.
South	Needs well-drained soil with pH above 5.5. Can be spring-planted in the North.
South	A good winter annual for the Southwest. Needs a pH of at least 6.
South	Less winter-hardy than hairy vetch and less suitable for sandy soil.
All	The most winter-hardy vetch and the best for most situations.
South	Better adapted to heavy, poorly drained soils than other vetches.
Gulf Coast	Least winter-hardy but produces more green material than other vetches.
All	Prefers pH 7 to 8. Spring varieties must be used in the North.
All	Plant in late summer and it will grow on into the winter. Can be eaten anytime.
All	Tolerates a wide pH range. Not good in heavy clay. Spring varieties must be used in the North.
All	Winter rye is the most hardy of the small grains and a very important winter cover crop.
All	One of the best winter cover crops. Grows rapidly in the fall. Dies before spring in the North and is easy to till under.
All	Prefers pH 7 to 8.5 and fertile soil. Winter variety is very cold-hardy.

Pit and Trench Composting

Burying garbage is a quick and easy way to recycle waste materials. Also called *pit composting*, it has the obvious advantage of putting everything out of sight and, for a while at least, out of mind. It also permits the composting material to stay warmer in the winter and damper in the summer.

On the farm, where pit composting is sometimes done on a fairly large scale, underground rotting allows bacteria, anaerobic fungus, and worms to transmute stinky masses of manure and litter into sweet-smelling soil. At home, if you throw debris into a hole that is 12 to 14 inches deep and cover it again with loose soil, it will decompose quite quickly.

Use a bucket to collect all those spent flower blossoms and weeds. Then, whenever it is full, dig a hole somewhere in your yard or garden and bury the material. You can also bury food scraps at the same time. Once it's decomposed, you can do one of two things: You can dig up the compost again and use it somewhere else, or you can plant a shrub, fruit tree, grapevine, or berry bush right over the pit.

Some folks with small gardens that are spaded and worked by hand bury garbage in long trenches. This is a good idea. Vegetable plantings can eventually be made directly on top of the covered trench, but it is not a healthy plan to do this too soon after the trench has been filled. It is better to allow the garbage plenty of time to decompose. Growing food in garbage that's too raw can cause stomach problems in humans. Root crops like beets, parsnips, rutabagas, and carrots may pick up some unpleasant parasites, which have not yet been destroyed by microbial activities, and then instill them in your intestinal tract.

Vertical Composting

The best trenching method involves a plan that I have heard called "vertical composting." You lay out your garden in 3-foot-wide rows, dividing each row into three 1-foot lanes. If you have

Year one: Dig a spade-width trench along the left-hand side of each 3-foot row. Leave the middle foot as a walkway — a narrow strip of mulch would not hurt here — and plant along the right-hand side of the section.

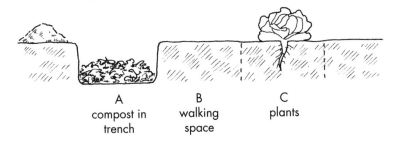

A	B	C
compost in trench	walking space	plants

Year two: Use the left-hand side as a walking space. Plant down the middle lane and trench-compost down the right side.

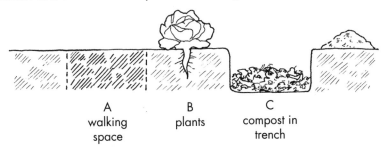

A	B	C
walking space	plants	compost in trench

Year three: Trench-compost in the center, walk on the right, and plant on the left where the underground garbage, buried during year one, has had a couple of full gardening seasons to rot.

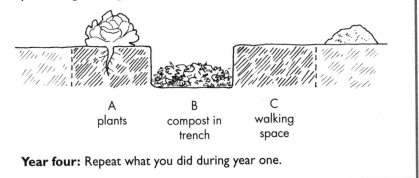

A	B	C
plants	compost in trench	walking space

Year four: Repeat what you did during year one.

doubts about your memory's ability to serve you well, keep records of what you have done each year in each 1-foot lane.

This is a simple yet systematic soil improvement program that permits you to bury your garbage right in the garden and still keep your stomach in good working order. There is no reason you cannot occasionally throw a bit of lime or wood ash into the trenches along with your vegetable scraps and other organic matter. This should keep your garden's soil somewhere near neutral.

Small-Scale Composting Systems

If you live on a small plot of land — or no land at all — you share a problem with millions of others. You and your family seem to produce a certain amount of organic waste, but you never seem to be able to scrounge up enough material to make a respectable-looking compost heap. There is no reason to feel cheated or to cop out on composting altogether. There are some easy composting alternatives that do not involve building large piles that heat up quickly and sustain high temperatures.

Earthworms

Earthworms — with a little help from you when it comes to some of the heavy work — will do a great job of making compost in a small pile that is only 1½ or 2 feet high. The succulent organic matter you put there will invite them from the ground below. You can even buy earthworms through the mail, if you like, and add them to your modest collection of grass clippings, leaves, and vegetable wastes.

Mail-order worms should not be confused with the kind of worms you might dig up or buy on the roadside for use as fishing bait. They are usually "compost worms" that have been bred and raised in the same sort of deliciously rich surroundings that your mini-pile will offer. These earthworms sport impressive names like Red Wiggler, Red Hybrid, or California Red, and they tend to be spoiled rotten, if you will excuse the expression. They have been so pampered and well fed that they will thrive *only* in your minigarden soil. To buy "reds" or "blue-gray thins," look for advertisements for earthworm companies in gardening magazines like *Horticulture* or *Organic Gardening* and mail-order gardening companies such as Gardener's Supply (see Sources). Once you have introduced a few earthworms into your pile, these "intestines of the soil," as they are sometimes called, will double their numbers in about a month's time.

INDOOR WORM COMPOSTING

You can also use earthworms to make compost out of your food scraps during the winter. All it takes is building a home for them and feeding them your leftovers. Mary Appelhof, worm-composting expert and author of *Worms Eat My Garbage,* recommends a wooden box 1 foot by 2 feet by 3 feet for food waste from a family of four (about 6 to 7 pounds of kitchen scraps per week). Plastic boxes of various sizes and shapes are often available from companies that sell composting supplies (see Sources).

Here are some suggestions to get you started:

1. Fill the box with a bedding of shredded newspapers, manure, or leaf mold.

2. Locate the box where temperatures stay above 50°F and below 84°F.

3. Add some redworms or others sold expressly for indoor composting. You'll need twice as many worms as the average daily amount of garbage you'll be asking them to process (i.e., if you generate ½ pound of garbage per day, you'll need 1 pound of worms).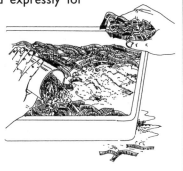

4. Feed them your food garbage daily, preferably ground up in a blender.

Worms' castings, which look very much like coffee grounds, are five times richer than the most fertile soil and loaded with microorganisms. The simplest method of removing the castings from the worm composter is to move the bedding and worms to one side of the box every two or three months and fill the other side with new bedding. Bury your garbage in the new bedding, and when worms have migrated to the new side, remove the castings from the other side. Use this precious compost as a top-dressing on potted plants and flower beds or as a potting and seed-starting medium, and add some to planting holes for flower and vegetable transplants. Brew up some castings tea by soaking a handful of castings in water and use it on your potted plants and young transplants.

Plastic Bag Composting

Garbage and nearly any other kind of organic matter can be decomposed in those green 32-gallon trash bags. The process is primarily anaerobic, but you can open the bag every day to let in

---

COMPOSTING IN A BAG

1. Toss in food scraps (chopped up in blender or food processor, if possible) leaves, grass clippings, some garden soil or bagged compost (to provide the necessary microbes), and a little alfalfa meal or pellets to activate the batch.

2. Shake the bag daily to mix up contents. Add water if needed, or add leaves or dried grass clippings if mixture is too wet.

3. Once bag is full, you can spread contents on your garden and start over. When you open the bag, be sure to take it out of the house first. Stand back, hold your nose, and dump the contents on the ground.

4. Spread and fluff the material so that it is exposed to lots of oxygen. Mix in some soil and let it sit for a day or two to dry out before mixing it into your garden.

---

some air. Best of all, there is absolutely no danger of leaching with this method.

Almost nothing in the way of microbial digestion will happen if the material in the bag gets too cold or freezes. This is why trash bag composting will not work outside or in an unheated barn, woodshed, or other outbuilding.

Compost Pit

I have often thought about modifying some of the compost pit ideas I have read about by building a concrete or concrete block compost pit in the side of a fairly steep hill. I know that compost containers that are sunk into the ground should have no bottoms, of course, and that they should have crushed stone or gravel near the base. Otherwise, water will have nowhere to drain, and after a heavy rain the compost would get soggy and smelly and there would be very little to prevent it from staying that way.

What would happen if you installed a drain in the bottom of a sunken compost container and ran a pipe to a lower basin further down the hill to collect the compost water, as shown in the drawing below? This fertile juice, or compost tea would be a treat for vegetable plants if it was used as a side-dressing and would provide wonderful nourishment for tiny plants in seed flats. It seems to me that this would be a near perfect system. Almost nothing would be lost through leaching.

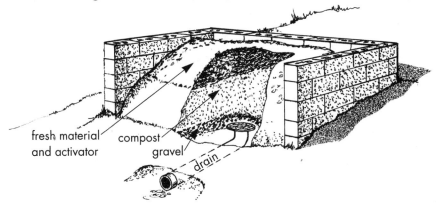

fresh material and activator   compost   gravel   drain

Composting Systems at a Glance

Type	Advantages	Disadvantages
Slow outdoor pile	Easy to start and add to; low maintenance.	Can take a year or more to decompose; nutrients are lost to leaching; can be odorous and attract animals and flies.
Hot outdoor pile	Fast decomposition; weed seeds and pathogens are killed; more nutrient-rich because less leaching of nutrients; less likely to attract animals and flies.	Requires lots of effort to turn and aerate and manage the process; works best when you have lots of material to add right away, as opposed to a little bit at a time.
Bin or box	Neat appearance; holds heat more easily than a pile; deters animals; lid keeps rain off compost; if turned, decomposition can be quite rapid.	Costs you time to build the bin or money to buy it.
Tumbler	Self-contained and not messy; can produce quick compost; relatively easy to aerate by turning the tumbler; odor not usually a problem; no nutrient leaching into ground.	Tumblers are costly; volume is relatively small; works better if material is added all at once.
Pit composting	Quick and easy; no maintenance; no investment in materials.	Only takes care of small amount of organic matter.

Type	Advantages	Disadvantages
Sheet-composting	Can handle large amounts of organic matter; no containers required; good way to improve soil in large areas.	Requires effort to till material into the soil; takes several months to decompose.
Plastic bag or garbage can	Easy to do year-round; can be done in a small space; can be done indoors; requires no back labor.	Is mostly anaerobic, so smell can be a problem; can attract fruit flies; need to pay attention to C/N ratio to avoid a slimy mess.
Worm composter	Easy; no odor; can be done indoors; can be added to continuously; so nutrient-rich it can be used as a fertilizer; good way to compost food waste.	Requires some care when adding materials and removing castings; need to protect worms from temperature extremes; can attract fruit flies.

Bins, Barrels, and Tumblers

Many gardeners ask, "Why do I need a bin or a box — why not just a pile?" Good question. A pile works fine if you have the time and the patience to build it carefully, shape it properly, and can continue to keep it correctly shaped after you have turned it or added more materials. The main advantage of the container is that you don't have to waste time tapering the pile to prevent it from becoming top-heavy and falling over. Containers also help keep your pile from looking unruly and provide some insulation against heat and moisture loss. The container can be as complicated as you are handy and imaginative. Or it can be a very simple thing if you are too busy to make something more elaborate.

The Wooden Box

Most compost containers — or "organizers," as they are sometimes called — are modifications of Sir Albert Howard's New
Zealand compost box. Sir Albert suggested the design for the
original box, which was built by a gardening club in Auckland,
New Zealand. Howard also wisely suggested that two boxes
side by side would yield the best results. His thought was that a
gardener could be building a pile in one bin as materials
became available while the second box, already filled with
organic matter, was left to ferment. (See page 50 for a discussion of the Indore process.)

The true New Zealand box is made of wood. The design
specifications, as were all of Sir Albert's directions, are precisely outlined. Besides assorted nuts, bolts, and washers, you
need:

- 6 pieces of 2" × 2", 3'3" long for uprights
- 24 pieces of 1" × 6" × 48" for the sides

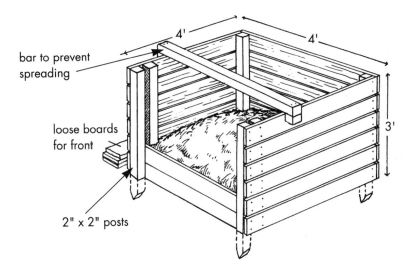

Drive the uprights into the ground to a depth of 3 inches. The sides, six boards to a side, should be bolted to the uprights around three sides (see illustration on page 73). Leave a ½-inch gap between each of the side boards to allow air into the pile.

The box has no top and no bottom and removable front boards; the 1" × 6" boards are not fastened by bolts, but can be slid in and out as needed to permit access to the pile. The dimensions of the base are 4 feet by 4 feet. It is 3 feet high and allows air circulation from all four sides. To keep the sides of the box from bulging out, Sir Albert recommended a crossbar with blocks on either side, which rests, unfastened, on top of the container.

There is actually no reason to take all of Howard's very exacting instructions to heart. You should consider the New Zealand box as a frame of reference from which you can design your own container. The dimensions of 4 feet by 4 feet are good ones for any home composting system, but a pile that is higher than 3 feet might be more desirable for heat retention. Wood is a perfectly satisfactory building material. Redwood, cedar, and cypress resist decay and will make a long-lasting box.

Sir Albert recognized that wood is biodegradable and saw a need for some sort of wood preservative. He also realized that creosote and tar would have a damaging effect on some of the organic matter in the pile and would be toxic to many microorganisms, insects, and earthworms. He recommended using motor oil as a preservative, but this is also toxic and should be avoided. I have been told that Cuprinol, a well-known commercial wood preserver, is all right to paint on a wooden compost frame. But the smell puts me off, and I have never dared try it on anything that was going to be touching plants. Water-based latex paint and linseed oil would be safe, and silicone-based preservatives are nontoxic.

Wire Bins

Wire mesh bins are easy to build out of fencing or chicken wire, or you can buy them from gardening supply companies. Wire containers tend to lose more heat than bins with more solid sides, so decomposition will be slower. You can use a plastic liner to help contain the heat. The advantage of a wire bin is that you can simply pick it up once the compost is ready and move it to a new location. Your compost pile is then easily accessible — no need to shovel material out of the top.

An easy-to-build wire bin consists of 2-by-6-inch boards covered with ½-inch chicken wire mesh. Make two L-shaped sections that hook together with hooks and eyes. To turn the pile, simply unhook the sides, lift them off the pile, and reassemble the bin next to the pile. Fork the materials into the empty bin.

CIRCULAR BIN (3½-FOOT DIAMETER)

Materials

12½ feet of 36" side 1" poultry wire, *or*

½" hardware cloth, *or*

18-gauge plastic-coated wire mesh,

4 metal or plastic clips, or copper wire ties

Three or four 4-foot wooden or metal posts to support wire

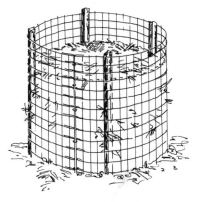

Circular bin

Tools

Heavy-duty wire or tin snips

Pliers

Hammer or metal file

Work gloves

Construction Details

Roll out and cut 12½ feet of poultry wire, hardware cloth, or plastic-coated wire mesh.

Poultry Wire:

1. If using poultry wire, roll back 3 to 4 inches at each end of cut piece to provide a strong, clean edge that will be easy to lath and won't poke or snag.
2. Set wire circle in place for compost pile and secure ends with clips or wire ties.
3. Space wood or metal posts around perimeter inside wire circle.
4. Pound posts firmly into the ground while tensing them against wire to provide support.

Hardware Cloth:

1. If using hardware cloth, trim ends flush with a cross wire to eliminate loose edges that may poke or scratch hands.
2. File each wire along cut edge to ensure safer handling when opening and closing bins.
3. Bend hardware cloth into circle and attach ends with clips or ties.

Set bin in place for composting. Bins made with hardware cloth should be strong enough to stand alone without posts. Plastic-coated wire mesh bins are made in the same manner, except that bending this heavier material into an even circular shape will require extra effort. Also, filing the wire ends may cause the plastic coating to tear. Striking the end of each wire with a hammer a few times will knock down any jagged edges.

Five-Panel Bin

Materials
15 feet of 24" wide 12- to 16-
gauge plastic-coated wire
mesh
20 metal or plastic clips, or
plastic-coated copper wire
ties

Tools
Heavy-duty wire or tin snips
Pliers
Hammer or metal file
Work gloves

Five-panel bin

Construction Details
Roll out and cut 12½ feet of poultry wire, hardware cloth,
or plastic-coated wire mesh.

Poultry Wire:
1. If using poultry wire, roll back 3 to 4 inches at each
   end of cut piece to provide a strong, clean edge that
   will be easy to lath and won't poke or snag.
2. Set wire circle in place for compost pile and secure
   ends with clips or wire ties.
3. Space wood or metal posts around perimeter inside
   wire circle.
4. Pound posts firmly into the ground while tensing
   them against wire to provide support.

Hardware Cloth:
1. If using hardware cloth, trim ends flush with a cross
   wire to eliminate loose edges that may poke or
   scratch hands.

2. Apply file to each wire along cut edge to ensure safer handling when opening and closing bins.
3. Bend hardware cloth into circle and attach ends with clips or ties.

Set bin in place for composting. Bins made with hardware cloth should be strong enough to stand alone without posts. Plastic-coated wire mesh bins are made in the same manner, except that bending this heavier material into an even circular shape will require extra effort. Also, filing the wire ends may cause the plastic coating to tear. Striking the end of each wire with a hammer a few times will knock down any jagged edges.

Construction Details

1. Cut five 3-foot-long sections of 24" wide wire mesh.
2. Make cuts at the top of the next row of squares to leave 1" long wires sticking out along one cut edge of each panel. This edge will be the top of the bin. Use a pair of pliers to bend over and tightly clamp each wire on this edge. This provides protection against scraping arms when adding yard wastes to the bin.
3. Attach panels using clips or wire ties.

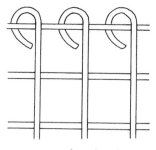

Top edge detail

Bin designs pp. 75–82 developed by Seattle Tilth Association for Seattle's Master Composter Program. Reprinted with permission from Seattle Tilth and the Seattle Engineering Department.

Wood and Wire Stationary Three-Bin System

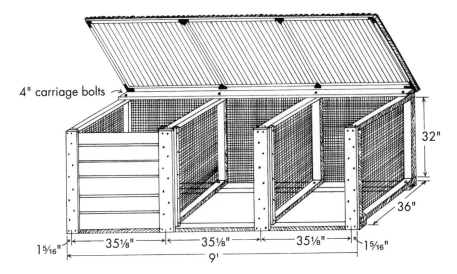

4" carriage bolts

32"

36"

1⁵⁄₁₆"   35⅛"   35⅛"   35⅛"   1⁵⁄₁₆"

9'

Materials

Two 18-foot treated 2 × 4s

Four 12-foot, or eight 6-foot treated 2 × 4s

One 9-foot and two 6-foot 2 × 2s

One 16-foot cedar 2 × 6

Nine 6-foot cedar 1 × 6s

22 feet of 36" wide ½" hardware cloth

12 ½" carriage bolts 4" long

12 washers and 12 nuts for bolts

3 lbs. of 16d galvanized nails

½ lb. 8d galvanized casement nails

250 poultry wire staples or power stapler w/ 1" staples

One 12-foot and one 8-foot sheet 4 oz. clear corrugated
fiberglass

Three 8-foot lengths of wiggle molding

40 gasketed aluminum nails for corrugated fiberglass
roofing

Two 3" zinc-plated hinges for lid

8 flat 4" corner braces with screws

4 flat 3" T-braces with screws

Tools

Hand saw or circular power saw
Drill with ½" and ⅛" bits
Screwdriver
Hammer
Tin snips
Tape measure
Pencil
¾" socket or open-ended wrench
Carpenter's square
Power stapler with 1" long galvanized staples (optional)
Safety glasses and ear protection

Construction Details

A. Build Dividers

1. Cut two 31½" and two 36" pieces from each 12-foot 2 × 4.
2. Butt end nail the four pieces into a 35" × 36" square. Repeat for other three sections.
3. Cut four 37" long sections of hardware cloth, bend back edges 1".
4. Stretch hardware cloth across each frame, check for square-ness of the frame, and staple screen tightly into place every 4" around edge.

Butt nail diagram

B. Set Up Dividers

1. Set up dividers parallel to one another 3 feet apart.
2. Measure and mark centers for the two inside dividers.
3. Cut four 9-foot pieces out of the two 18-foot 2 × 4 boards.

4. Place two 9-foot base boards on top of dividers and measure the positions for the two inside dividers.
5. Mark a center line for each divider on the 9-foot 2 × 4.
6. With each divider, line up the center lines and make the base board flush against the outer edge of the divider.
7. Drill a ½" hole through each junction centered 1" in from the inside edge.
8. Secure base boards with carriage bolts, but do not tighten yet.
9. Turn the unit right side up and repeat the process for the top 9-foot board.
10. Using the carpenter's square or measuring between opposing corners, make sure the bin is square, and tighten all bolts securely.
11. Fasten a 9-foot-long piece of hardware cloth securely to the back side of the bin with staples every 4" around the frame.

C. Front Slats and Runners
1. Cut four 36" long 2 × 6s for front slat runners.
2. Rip-cut two of these boards to 4¾" wide and nail them securely to the front of the outside dividers and baseboard, making them flush on top and outside edges. Save remainder of rip-cut boards for use as back runners.
3. Center the remaining full width dividers flush with the top edge, and nail securely.
4. To create back runners, cut the remaining 2 × 6 into a 34" long piece and then rip cut into four equal pieces, 1¼" × 2".
5. Nail back runners parallel to front runners on side of divider leaving a 1" gap for slats.
6. Cut all the 1 × 6 cedar boards into slats 31¼" long.

D. Fiberglass Lid

1. Use the last 9-foot 2 × 4 for the back of the lid.
2. Cut four 32½ inch 2 × 2s and one 9-foot 2 × 2.
3. Lay out into position on ground as illustrated and check for squareness.
4. Screw in corner braces and T-braces on bottom side of the frame.
5. Center lid frame, brace side down, on bin structure and attach with hinges.
6. Cut wiggle board to fit the front and back 9-foot sections of the lid frame.
7. Predrill wiggle board with ⅛" drill bit and nail with 8d casement nails.
8. Cut fiberglass to fit flush with front and back edges.
9. Overlay pieces at least one channel wide.
10. Predrill fiberglass and wiggle board for each nail hole.
11. Nail on top of every third hump with gasketed nails.

Commercial Plastic Bins

If you don't have the space and time to build an outdoor bin, consider one of the ready-made enclosed containers on the market. An enclosed plastic bin offers the advantage of quick setup and attractive appearance. The container has no bottom, so you can set it directly on the ground. You can add materials, turn the pile, and aerate by opening the lid. When compost is ready, you can scoop it out of a bottom opening. Most of these bins have the disadvantage of containing less than 1 cubic yard of materials, which is the minimum size often recommended for hot composting. The walls do help hold the heat in, however, and I wouldn't hesitate to use one to dispose of leaves, grass clippings, and food wastes. I'd be sure to add enough nitrogenous materials to activate the process and boost the heat, and I'd chop or shred any brush to help speed things along. If all goes well, you can get compost in about a month.

Barrels, Drums, and Cans

With a little know-how and the right tools, you can turn steel drums, barrels, and garbage cans into composters. Following are instructions for some different types.

STEEL DRUM COMPOSTER

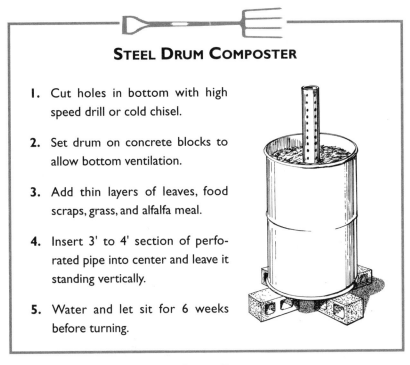

1. Cut holes in bottom with high speed drill or cold chisel.

2. Set drum on concrete blocks to allow bottom ventilation.

3. Add thin layers of leaves, food scraps, grass, and alfalfa meal.

4. Insert 3' to 4' section of perforated pipe into center and leave it standing vertically.

5. Water and let sit for 6 weeks before turning.

GARBAGE CAN COMPOSTER

Variation A
1. Remove base with coping saw or portable jigsaw.
2. Lay piece of chicken wire or hardware cloth on bricks or 2 × 4.
3. Set can on top of screen.
4. Put 4" of dry, coarse material in bottom, then add layers of food scraps, alfalfa meal, leaves, wood ashes, and a little soil.
5. Keep materials moist.

Variation B
1. Use intact garbage can. Drill several rows of air holes in bottom and sides of can.
2. Add materials and securely fasten lid.
3. Once a day, roll can around to mix contents.

Variation C
1. Use intact garbage can. Drill several rows of holes in bottom and sides.
2. Dig hole 15" deep and diameter of can in a location accessible from kitchen or back door. (If soil isn't well-drained, mix in some sand ahead of time.)
3. Set can in hole and firm soil around sides.
4. Add food scraps as they accumulate, topping each layer with shredded newspapers, straw, or leaves.

Tumblers

Compost tumblers are commercially available in various sizes and shapes. They are more expensive than most other types of containers. Some consist of a plastic barrel suspended on a stand to facilitate turning of the entire barrel. The sides have holes for aeration; the lid comes off to add materials and dump out compost. Some units are many-sided and can be rolled around on the ground to mix the materials. These tumblers are easy to set up and fairly easy to turn even when full. But some of them hold less than 1 cubic yard, and some compost experts believe the tumbling facilitates dry-rotting and loss of nitrogen rather than proper thermophilic decomposition. Others argue that if you add chopped material all at once and include manure or soil or finished compost as an activator, in about a month you can get compost that will greatly improve your soil's structure.

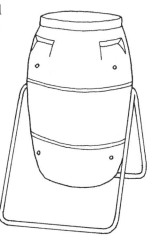

More Ideas

Circular Bins

A rectangular container with corner posts is a little easier to build than a round one. However, a circular bin is ideal because it allows a maximum amount of air to penetrate all parts of the pile. Circular containers can be made with wire mesh, snow fencing, pickets, or hardware cloth. Leonard Wickenden, in his book *Gardening with Nature*, suggests building a pile in the shape of a doughnut. This hole-in-the-middle design would allow for almost perfect aeration. One possible problem posed by the design is that you would louse the whole thing up each time you had to turn the pile and would have to spend a lot of time rebuilding. Of course, in a pile with such a shape, turning could be less frequent. I have yet to see a doughnut-shaped container on the market.

Block Bins

I have seen containers made with fieldstone drywalls and have built containers myself out of cinder blocks like the one shown. A stable 4-foot block wall can be made easily without using any mortar. If you lay the blocks on their sides, the holes will provide excellent ventilation. The advantage of any stone or concrete block wall is that it retains heat from the sun and will keep the compost warm for a while as the air temperature drops.

Bale Bins

Bales of hay make good retaining walls, and the hay itself can be gradually incorporated into the pile. A bale of hay has a lot of insulation value. In Vermont, hay has long been used to "bank" the foundations of homes to keep out cold winter winds. Insulate your pile with hay bales, allowing the hay to weather as it sits outside all winter (weathered hay, by the way, makes excellent mulch), and keep a ready supply of new compost material right on the compost site. Sod walls are another possibility. I have seen this work beautifully, but this kind of pile gets little air and needs to be turned often.

Creative Bins

A short log cabin-type structure makes an attractive box. You might try bricks or lattice or picket fencing, too. Wooden pallets are handy because they have spaces between the slats for ventilation.

It's not within the scope of this book to give precise directions for building all the different types of structures you can use to contain your compost, mainly because there's no limit to what your imagination can dream up. Nor do I want you to think I have covered all the compost containers and supplies on the market, because by the time this book is published there will be new products available. Visit your local garden centers. Write to the mail-order sources listed in the back of this book. Look around and see what other people are using. Perhaps your state Extension Service or local solid waste department has some suggestions.

What to Consider Before Building a Compost Pile

Even today, compost piles have a bad reputation. In many places, it is still believed that they invite dogs and other pests, are the homes of mice, rats, and snakes, and are iniquitous breeding dens for flies, mosquitoes, and similar undesirable insects. Granted that dogs and rats may be a problem in some urban and suburban areas, the tales of devastation wrought by dogs and stories of rat-infested compost are grossly exaggerated. I have never seen a snake anywhere near a compost pile. Nor have we been plagued by bugs that were born out of our compost.

We have a frisky German shepherd who, from the very beginning, along with a multitude of her friends, have all regarded our compost pile with intense boredom — when they have paid any attention to it at all. We feed *her* our meat scraps — not the pile. Chicken bones or fish bones, which she should not have anyway, are ground up fine and placed deep in the pile together with the other garbage. I am sure that if kitchen wastes were just thrown on top of the heap without being covered with a thick layer of hay, she would smell it and be far more interested.

As it is, none of the neighborhood dogs has ever, to my knowledge, disturbed our compost pile at all. In fact, on a cold autumn night not long ago our shepherd was either too lazy to ask to come inside the house, or one of us was simply too lazy to let her in. As I was scraping frost from the car's windshield early the next morning, I heard the thump-thump of her tail and turned to see her returning my amused look from atop the warm compost pile, where she had apparently spent a comfortable night without realizing there was something edible directly beneath her.

Fortunately, we have no rats around our place, but I am constantly trying to invent ways to outsmart a large tribe of raccoons that lives nearby and raids our trash cans nightly. The dog and I both carry on a losing battle with them — I with assorted ropes, weights, and other devices; she chiefly with loud nocturnal barking. She is particularly annoyed when they become bold enough not only to steal her dog food but to wash it first in her water dish. The raccoons are forever in the trash, yet they seem to have no interest at all in the compost. If you have something of a pest problem where you live, the

difficulty can probably be resolved by using some kind of cover (chicken wire, perhaps) to protect your pile. More on that later.

Maintaining the Proper Appearance

In years past, people held rather strict Victorian attitudes toward composting. Whenever I see someone's compost pile tucked surreptitiously away in some corner of their property hidden by a screen or hedge, I am inevitably reminded of my great-grandmother on my mother's side. One time my mother, as a young child, was sitting in a hallway as that fine lady made her grand exit from her marble bathroom. "Hi Grandma, have you been to the potty?" my mother asked. "My dear," replied my great-grandmother looking down, "grandmothers never go to the bathroom!" In her day, undoubtedly, the "right" sort of people never made compost, either.

Today, compost and going to the bathroom seem to have become more acceptable and less clandestine facts of life. In fact, attitudes have become so liberal over the past couple of decades that now some people regard their compost piles as status symbols. It seems a little unnecessary, as happened to my wife and me recently, to take dinner guests by the hand and hustle them out to observe your compost heap. Your pile need not be hidden, nor in the most plainly visible spot on your land. Choose its locale carefully. There are other factors to consider that are more important than appearance.

Locating Your Pile

Obviously, you will want to have your compost pile as close as possible to the garden proper so that you don't have to lug or cart materials back and forth over a long distance. If you own a pickup truck or similar vehicle that can help you bring in organic materials from other places, perhaps you should plan to build your composting system near a driveway or road. The pile does not need to be too near the house itself. Moreover, you don't want it sitting directly under dripping eaves or downspouts, which can dump an uncontrollable amount of water on it.

Your bin or pile should be near a water source, though — at least within reach of your garden hose. Some folks, because they worry about chlorine in a municipal water system, go to great lengths to catch and collect pure rainwater to use on their compost. Chlorine can conceivably cause some damage to the microcommunity in the pile, but I use chlorinated water all the time, both on my compost pile and on the garden, and I haven't noticed any ill effects. You can neutralize the chlorine in the water by letting it sit in an open container for a day or two before you use it.

Should your pile be located in the sun or the shade? If you live in a cold climate, you may want the help of the sun's heat to warm your pile, but you'll have to be prepared to add water so it doesn't dry out. In a warmer climate you can locate the pile in the shade, where it won't dry out so quickly. If you have the foresight, it would be ideal to locate your pile on a future garden spot so the nutrients that leach from the pile into the ground will be put to good use later. These are only guidelines, though. Locate the pile wherever it's most convenient and where you are sure to tend it.

A fairly standard bit of advice is that the pile should be protected on the north, east, and west sides by some sort of wall, hedge, or container, and that the south side, if possible, should be left open. The best reason for this would seem to be to protect the pile from cold winds, while at the same time allowing the sun to reach it directly and keep it warmer. This is a particularly good idea in some places, such as Alaska, where I understand it takes two to three years to make compost under the best circumstances. In most climates, though, the way the compost is situated probably isn't that important.

What Kind of Foundation?

Many people think it's best to have the pile in direct contact with bare ground. In fact, some people dig down a couple of feet to establish the base of the pile. I wouldn't care to go that far, but I might dig up the sod and lay it aside for later use in, or on top of, the pile. The idea here is to give the microorganisms and earthworms maximum opportunity to find their way into the compost from the soil below. If you are too busy to dig up the sod, don't worry. It will disappear in a few months anyway.

If you use this method, don't move your composting site around if you can help it. Keeping the pile in the same spot year after year helps the earth beneath to accumulate a large population of microorganisms and spores. When the pile is finally carted away to the garden and a new pile is started, the remaining bacteria and fungi can start right in on it. Leave a little finished compost on the site to act as a "culture" for the new heap of organic matter.

Drainage

Drainage can be something of a problem. I have often heard the suggestion made that a pile should be located in a depression to prevent the loss of nutrients through leaching. That sounds like a good idea except that a low place often means standing water, or at best, such good drainage under the soil in the depression that nutrients are going to drain away anyway. In other words, if you want your compost pile in a puddle, this is fine, but the result may be that you end up with a smelly, anaerobic mess. I would say that ideally a pile should be on a level spot where drainage is reasonably good.

Raised Piles

Another approach is to build the pile several inches above the ground. This enhances aeration in the pile by creating air channels from below. You can make a base of wire or wooden pallets. Don't raise the pile too far above the ground, though, or the air beneath will cool the pile down and slow decomposition. With this method, you're trading off the advantage of contact with the earth for enhanced aeration. On the one hand, if your pile has a good variety of organic materials and some finished compost or garden soil, it probably already contains the necessary soil organisms, and your pile needn't be in contact with the ground. On the other hand, if you create plenty of air channels throughout your pile as you build it, raising the pile off the ground isn't necessary. Your particular situation will dictate which approach makes more sense for you. If you love experimenting, build two piles, trying both methods to discover which works best for you.

A raised pile allows air to be pulled up from the bottom and through the pile.

Some Things to Avoid

Some sticklers for neatness like to build their piles on concrete or blacktop slabs. This provides a neat work space and prevents nutrients from being leached into the ground beneath the pile. But this approach both impedes aeration beneath the pile and inhibits microbial contact with the earth. If at all possible, avoid this method.

Some people have suggested laying an impervious film of polyethylene plastic on the ground before starting to build a pile. The theory is that this will trap whatever nutrients may leach out of the pile. Certain nutrients — potassium (potash), for example — will wash out of compost quite easily. But again, if by trying to retain a little potash (which can easily be replaced by adding wood ashes to the pile) you cut off the oxygen supply and make the pile less accessible to soil organisms, you are in effect robbing Peter to pay Paul. Laying plastic, as well as building a pile in a swamp or on a concrete slab, is a questionable practice.

How Big Should a Pile Be?

If you want hot, fast compost, your pile should measure at least 1 cubic yard. A pile that is too small will have a hard time heating up and will cool off, or even freeze, quite readily. In most areas of the continental United States, a compost pile needs quite a bit of mass to be self-insulating and maintain ideal temperatures. A pile that is too small may lose its heat so quickly each night that pathogenic organisms, weed seeds, and larvae will not be killed, slowing the whole process.

On the other hand, a pile that's too large can have different problems. The length doesn't matter, but if you make it much wider or higher than 5 or 6 feet, the center of the pile may not get enough air and you could wind up with an anaerobic area there. Air naturally penetrates anywhere from 18 to 24 inches into a pile from all directions, but not much beyond that. The center of the pile can heat up too much, killing off the microorganisms. You're apt to overheat yourself as well if you try turning a huge heap (more on turning in chapter 9). Try to keep your pile between 4 and 6 feet high.

Layering Materials in the Pile

You can construct the pile as materials become available to you, or you can wait until you've accumulated lots of organic material before you begin. Autumn is often the most convenient time to start a new pile, after you've pulled up old vegetable plants, raked the leaves, and completed your fall cleanup.

If you have lots of material to start with, try to build your pile like a Dagwood sandwich, in many layers, using as many ingredients as you can get your hands on. Alternate "green" layers of fresh vegetable matter with "dry" layers of weathered material, absorbent layers with wet layers, carbon materials with nitrogen materials. Try not to let one kind of material get concentrated in any part of the pile. An old standby formula might be: a 6-inch layer of vegetable matter, a second 6-inch layer of different vegetable matter, a layer of some sort of animal matter (such as manure), a thin layer of soil or finished compost, and water; the process is then repeated.

This formula can easily be adapted and changed. You may choose not to have any kind of animal matter and instead use another natural activator. You may use sprinklings of rock powders such as rock phosphate. I'll leave you to experiment.

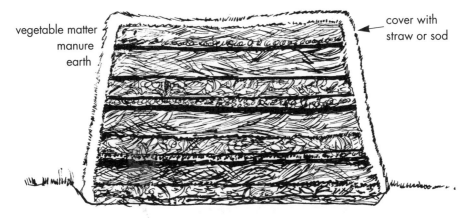

vegetable matter
manure
earth

cover with
straw or sod

Remove sod and replace with coarse layer of gravel or brush, and repeat vegetable matter, manure, and earth pattern.

As decomposition really gets under way, the pile will shrink anywhere from 20 to 60 percent, depending on the materials that have been put into it. Add a new layer of material to increase the height again, if you'd like. What better way to reduce the volume of your yard waste!

Insulation

As the pile approaches a height of around 4½ feet, begin to give some thought to insulation. You will have to make your pile bulkier if it is to function at optimum efficiency throughout the winter. (Activity will slow down, but you can "winter over" the pile successfully in most any climate.) The idea is to keep the pile as operational as possible for as long as possible during the coldest months. A heavy layer of straw, hay, or leaves will insulate your pile. A waterproof cover is another possibility, as long as it isn't resting directly on top of the pile. A burlap or canvas "blanket" is almost as effective as leaves or straw. It will allow some water and gases through and still keep the pile warm.

Methods to Speed
Decomposition

Composting can be a fascinating diversion most of the time. If you are like me, you may find it almost impossible not to visit your compost pile each day, push some of the top material aside, and have a look at what is going on inside. This sort of fascination is a kind of addiction, I guess, but a healthy one as far as the natural order of things is concerned.

The other day, a self-sufficient neighbor of mine (who grows almost all of his own food to feed a family of five) was telling me about his father, a well-known figure in New York publishing circles. He is totally unlike his son in that he is completely dependent on the supermarket for food and other necessities. "I don't think Dad has ever grown a vegetable in his life. He doesn't have the time or the space, really. But he has always been interested in gardening. He's been giving me books about it ever since I was about six. And you know, for as long as I can remember he has always had a compost pile in his little backyard!" I wondered what he did with all his compost once it was finished. My friend replied, "I think he gives it to a neighbor who grows championship roses." This man is a purist, one of the most dedicated composters I have ever heard about.

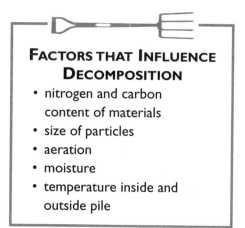

FACTORS THAT INFLUENCE DECOMPOSITION

- nitrogen and carbon content of materials
- size of particles
- aeration
- moisture
- temperature inside and outside pile

Obviously, composting has its rewards: spiritual, as in the case of this very literate man, and earthly, in the form of that rich, black humus, which can do our greens so much good. Neither of these benefits, unfortunately, comes without a certain amount of effort. To properly build, water, and turn a pile takes a little work.

If your primary goal in composting is to reduce the volume of your leaves, brush, prunings, and food scraps, you may be content to pile up the materials and let nature take over the work. If you're after the final product to improve your soil, you'll probably be willing to invest more energy in the process.

This chapter should help hurry nature along a bit. Once you understand why some of these laborious tasks are necessary, they may become a little more fun and a little less tedious.

Aeration

We've talked about how essential good aeration is to the process of decomposition in your compost pile. You can create enough air passages if you give it some thought before you build. Once your pile is 4 feet high, it's a little late. Even if you don't raise the pile off the ground, you can create air channels on the bottom by making the first layer with coarse material such as light brush or hedge trimmings. Adding 2 to 4 inches of sunflower stalks also works like a charm because they have soft centers that rot out quickly, providing air channels.

You can also build your pile around ventilating stacks made of perforated drainage pipe (this is the stuff that is laid beneath gravel around the perimeter of new houses), wire mesh twisted into cylinders, or cornstalks.

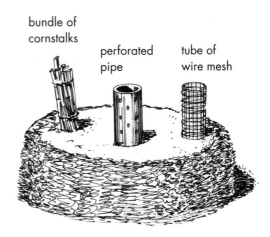

Ventilating stacks

Once your pile is built, you can try poking a piece of metal pipe down into the pile to open up a tunnel for oxygen, or try one of the tools on the market specifically designed to aerate your pile by lifting and fluffing the material. Be warned: If your pile contains lots of tough, fibrous material it can seem impenetrable. You'll just have to experiment to see if such tools will work for you.

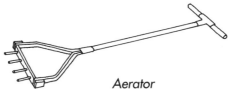

Aerator

Moisture

The amount of water in your compost pile is fairly critical, but you have plenty of leeway in which to work. If the moisture content is much greater than 60 percent, you run the risk of having an anaerobic pile; if it is much less than 40 percent, organic matter will not decompose rapidly enough because the bacteria are deprived of the moisture they need to carry on their metabolism. Of course, you can't monitor the percentages, so in general try to make sure the materials in your pile have the moisture content of a well-wrung sponge.

Getting It All Wet

Your biggest problem, as I see it, will be getting enough moisture to all parts of the pile. I have heard it said that the moisture content must be about right if the surface particles in the pile "glisten" with wetness. This is more than a little misleading. Soaking a pile with a garden hose until water runs off it does not necessarily mean that water is sinking through to all of the lower layers. In fact, squirting water on the surface might do no more than moisten the top 1 inch of material.

Sometimes, if water gets only to its outer layers, a pile will dry out faster! The outer surfaces can cake — preventing both water and air penetration. If this seems to have happened in your pile, you might try pricking some holes for water percolation as well as aeration. Even if you do, when it comes time to turn the pile you may be disappointed to discover small pockets of dry material where little decay has been going on. In the long run, you may also find that you have to dismantle the pile somewhat and add water here and there if you have a serious drought problem.

Moisten As You Build

The best solution is to moisten the pile as you build it. If it is properly moistened to begin with, it is likely to stay that way. Again, fresh green materials, particularly those that have been chopped or shredded, should need little or no added moisture. Dry hay, sawdust, straw, peat moss, or corncobs should be thoroughly moistened before they go into the pile.

DID YOU KNOW?

Lettuce has a moisture content of 87 percent. Newspaper, 5 percent.

If you have the right kind of nozzle on your garden hose, dampen each new layer with a gentle spray. A real blast of water is not too effective and may disrupt the structure of the pile below. If you see water running out of the bottom of the pile, you are overwatering and are doing little more than leaching out some of the valuable nutrients you are trying so hard to collect.

Rainwater

Rainwater is the best kind to put on compost. It picks up lots of oxygen, minerals, and microorganisms as it falls through the air, giving your compost an added boost. Don't forget that you can "dish" the top of your pile to collect rainwater. Unpolluted pond water is good, too. Some people throw dishwater on their heaps. This may contain some good organic matter, but it also has detergents and grease, which may coat some of the vegetable matter, preventing aeration and inhibiting decomposition. Dishwater, no. Cooking water, yes! (Unless, of course, you are going to save it for soups, stews, or further cooking.)

If you build your compost pile out in the open, you can use a tarp or build a cover to regulate the amount of rainwater your pile receives. In a rainy climate, your pile could get waterlogged. Make sure whatever cover you fashion is not resting directly on top of the pile or it will cut off the air flow. Support the cover several inches above the pile. The easiest way — if you want your pile to be in the shade — is to stretch some hardware cloth between several trees and staple it securely in place.

When all else fails, use good common sense when it comes to watering. Reach partway into the pile in various spots and feel what is going on. If it is warm there and feels more or less like a squeezed-out sponge, everything is probably in great shape.

Turning

Turning your pile is the only "bummer" — the only real chore in the whole business of compost making. A cubic yard of finished compost weighs about 800 to 1100 pounds; compost-in-the-making weighs slightly less. If you are inclined that way, you can figure out beforehand how much weight you are going to have to lift. Leonard Wickenden reminds us, reassuringly, that *without* turning compost at all, nature will take its course just as it always has. This is grist for your mill if you are good at rationalizing about *not* going through the effort of reorganizing your pile. But turning is worth the sweat: It decreases decomposition time. And this is, after all, one of the things composting is all about.

CAN'T WORMS DO THE WORK?

Unfortunately, you cannot rely on earthworms and other macroorganisms to do much of the turning for you. Earthworms are great workers. So are ants, mites, and other insects. But because worms are weak "pushers," they must literally eat their way through the materials in the pile. They do a lot of good things but cannot bring the "outside of the heap to the inside and the top to the bottom" the way you can with a five- or six-tined pitchfork — unless, of course, you have discovered a breed of particularly gifted worms. Inoculating the pile with earthworms in the hope they will do your turning for you is a waste of time.

In comparison with earthworms, ants are the real muscle men. They can move materials around like mad. But a well-watered pile is unlikely to have many ants. So worms and bugs can only do a little bit of mixing and reorganizing for you, mostly in the perimeter of the heap.

How Often?

How often you turn your pile depends largely on how ambitious you are. In general, it would seem that the more turning you do, the faster rotting will take place. But this is true only to a certain point. As you turn, you are mixing well-rotted materials with fresh, green material and wet stuff with dry stuff. All of this speeds decay. If a pile is turned too often, microorganisms will not have a chance to get much done. Each time you disturb the pile, you are killing a few microorganisms and their work is slowed down temporarily.

The temperature in your pile might help you decide how often you should turn it. If a pile has a good carbon/nitrogen ratio (discussed in chapter 4) and is composed of ground or chopped material (we'll talk about this next), it could reach a temperature peak of 150°F as often as every three or four days. You might want to turn it that often if you are intent on having a thermophilic pile. Normally, though, the cycle is longer than that. If you intend to keep track of the temperature to keep your pile at maximum heating capacity, turn the pile whenever your thermometer tells you that the temperature has dropped below about 100°F. But using temperature as your sole guide for turning means a lot of careful monitoring.

Most casual composters are content to achieve thermophilic temperatures that last for only a few days. This is usually enough time for a satisfactory thermal kill. Later, they allow the pile to cool off as the mesophiles take over and perform their good work. When this happens, pathogenic spores and weed seeds may survive for a while — at least until the pile is turned again and more heat is generated. Many home compost piles can be turned as infrequently as every six weeks to three months, unless the compost suddenly seems to be giving off a lot of odor.

Improve Oxygen Flow

Aside from affecting the rate of decomposition, turning also can remedy certain problems in your pile. A lack of oxygen can cause anaerobic conditions inside the pile, which can result in a foul odor. Also, an excess of nitrogenous materials can cause an ammonia smell to emanate from your pile. Turning your pile brings in the needed oxygen and lets the ammonia escape. Turn it, every day if you can, until the odor dissipates.

Another symptom of an anaerobic pile is layers of bluish gray mold (not the gray cobwebs of actinomycetes). Turning and fluffing the organic matter will get rid of the mold.

Tips on Turning

The most efficient way to turn your heap and see that the organic matter gets thoroughly remixed is to cut down the size of the pile in vertical slices. An ordinary spade works best for this if the ingredients in the pile are not too stringy. (If they are, it is best to use a pitchfork.)

The easiest kind of pile to turn is one inside a removable compost container. You can dismantle it, set it up again right next to the old pile, and move old material to the new location. Lots of composters who have permanent multicontainer systems try to schedule things so that the compost from one full container can be turned into an empty one right next to it. You may find that trying to turn a pile within a single container becomes a frustrating sort of haphazard process. You can never be quite sure about what you have turned and what you have not. But don't worry about exactitude. As long as you're mixing the materials, you're doing some good!

Grinding, Chopping, Chipping

Some organic matter will break down very slowly unless it's chopped up. Brush, sticks, heavy stems of cabbage and broccoli, tomato and pumpkin vines, cornstalks, and wet matted leaves all should be ground up, shredded, chopped, or chipped into smaller pieces. This increases the surface area that the microorganisms have to work on and speeds decomposition. Chopping materials also reduces the bulk of the organic matter. A pile of wood chips is far more compact than a pile of brush. You can put up to four times as many chopped leaves into a compact container as you could whole ones in the same place.

Chopping also bruises, cuts, tears, or punctures the tough outer skin of some types of vegetable matter and allows bacteria to get at the inner tissue. A fresh apple in a compost heap will soon become a rotten apple, turning brown and soft quite quickly, but unless its outer skin is cut or dented it will take a long time to rot completely.

Grinding or shredding breaks down the cell walls of plant tissue, too. Cellulose (the stuff that cell walls are made of) is hard to break down, so grinding helps here. Moisture will ooze from the microscopic plant cells that are broken, making the material moist. This, of course, can have an effect on the moisture content of the compost pile.

Ideally, you should have some control over the fineness or coarseness of the stuff that your chopping device produces. In the same way that green materials chopped too fine will make nothing but a green, pulpy mess, dry materials ground too fine will blend together when mixed with water to form a paste, which can dry and form a barrier that is impervious to water and air. This could happen, for example, with the small particles of sawdust produced by a belt sander. Be sure that this sawdust isn't concentrated in one section of the pile.

Everyday Equipment

An ordinary kitchen blender is a handy tool for preparing kitchen waste and garbage for composting. Just keep some sort of closed container (a large coffee can with a plastic lid works fine) on a back corner of the countertop. You can throw all of your compostable garbage into it and when you've accumulated a full container blend it up with a little water. Pour this wet slurry onto your pile, spreading it around so that it doesn't all wind up in the same spot.

Think of all the organic goodies that people feed to their garbage disposals instead of their soil. At least one avid home composter has fashioned a food-grinding apparatus using a garbage disposal unit. I don't have explicit directions, but if you're handy, try mounting the unit in a box instead of under the sink, add your food scraps (cutting up fibrous materials before adding them) and a little water, and collect the ground-up food in a bucket. If you're no Rube Goldberg, by the time you read this I'm sure there will be such a product on the market.

The cheapest and simplest chopper/chipper is a machete. They are usually available from army surplus stores, and it should be easy to find a stump or old plank to use as a chopping block. But you know the old saying about how chopping your own wood warms you twice, once by the exertion and once by burning the fruits of your labor? It seems to me that using a machete to chop up a lot of debris and leaves would heat you up a lot more than necessary. Still, a lot of people build good compost piles this way.

A rotary lawn mower can serve as a pretty good shredder. Lay whatever it is you want to chop on the ground and run the machine back and forth over it several times. You can even chop up sticks this way. Be sure that you aim the open end or chute toward some sort of backstop, such as a wall or a piece of plywood propped against a cart. If you don't, you'll have trouble gathering up the shredded material that is blown out of the mower.

Chippers and Shredders

The best tool for the job is, of course, the one designed to do exactly what the task calls for. There are lots of different kinds of chippers and shredders on the market, and you may decide that you generate enough compostable stuff to warrant such a purchase. Choose one compatible with the size of your property, your composting ambitions, and your garden's needs. Be sure to pick a machine that's ruggedly built. All choppers are subject to tremendous vibrations, and some fall apart too quickly.

Electric machines seem to be a good deal less powerful than their gasoline-powered cousins. They have the added disadvantage of requiring electrical outlets and heavy extension cords.

Choose a machine that is easy for you to move around; you may have to move it more than you think. Take some time to examine the mechanism that actually shreds the material. Find out if and how well you can regulate the size of the particles in the aggregate you will be making. Most good machines have a series of removable rods, screens, or grates that help you regulate the texture of the material coming out.

If the price tag of the machine you like is scaring you off, consider sharing one with your neighbors. The best ones can handle the composting chores of several families.

10

Composting Concerns

A n expert in any field, it seems, is a little like an octopus. You can follow him or her through familiar waters for just so long and then suddenly — and often unwittingly — he or she will hide behind an inkscreen of indecipherable statistics, jargon, formulae, or other jabberwocky. Sophisticated gardeners and highly technical composting experts are no exception. After a certain point they can become difficult, if not impossible, to understand. You and I can become the same if we are not careful.

At first, as a totally inexperienced gardener, I was easily bugged by gardening and composting literature that would throw terms like C/N, pH, and NPK at me. I wanted to know immediately how to make compost or grow peas. I didn't think I needed complicated explanations as to why. The temptation in situations like this is to write off the things we do not understand. It's easy to shrug and say, "I won't worry about it," when in fact what you are being told is important and is something you should worry about. So in this chapter, I'll try to help you understand some things you probably haven't thought about and dispel your fears about others.

pH

If you know nothing else about your garden soil, you should know its pH. Plants will literally be poisoned if the pH is much too high or low. The pH of the compost you put into the garden will have a marked effect on the soil there. Hence, it is a good idea to have some understanding of what pH is all about.

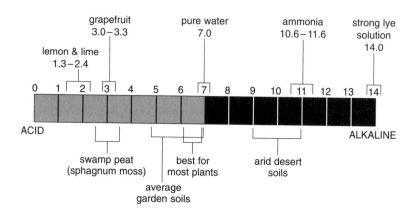

The pH scale and some commonly known substances

The term pH, as you may or may not recall from high school chemistry, describes the alkalinity ("sweetness") or acidity ("sourness") of soil, compost, and other substances, and pH is usually expressed as a number. The pH scale runs from 1, indicating pure acidity, to 14, which is purely alkaline or "basic." Something neutral would be described as 7, halfway between 1 and 14. The neutral zone, somewhere around 7, is desirable for most plants. Most bacteria and fungi operate best in a medium with a pH from 6.5 to slightly more than 7. Clearly, then, you want to keep your compost pile within this range.

You can find out the pH of your compost by having it analyzed. Send a sample to your state university Extension

Service just the way you would send a soil sample, or send it to a private soil-testing laboratory. Or, you can test it yourself with a home soil test kit, though the accuracy of these tests varies (in general, the simpler they are, the less accurate they tend to be); many gardening catalogs and garden centers carry them.

Keep in mind, though, that decaying compost naturally goes through a normal pH cycle. In the earliest stages of decomposition, the material tends to become acidic. If you were to do a pH test only a couple of weeks after activating the pile, you might get a distorted reading.

Later on, a healthy pile will neutralize itself on its own, as long as it is getting enough oxygen. As a matter of fact, it is probably safe to say that building and maintaining an aerobic pile that is made up of a wide variety of organic matter will almost automatically result in compost with a pH very close to 7. If the major portion of the pile is composed of some highly acidic materials such as oak leaves, pine needles, or pine sawdust, the resulting compost could be on the acid side. The best time to evaluate pH, however, is once the compost has been added to the soil. An alkaline soil amended with an acidic compost could provide near-neutral growing conditions for your plants.

Lime

Lime raises the pH of the material to which it is added, making it more alkaline. For this reason, some people like to add lime to compost made with acidic materials, such as pine needles, or when aerobic conditions predominate in the pile (anaerobes can lower the pH). But lime is best added to your soil after you've mixed in compost and verified pH with a soil test. When added directly to the compost, lime can cause nitrogen loss and suppress biological activity.

APPROXIMATE COMPOSITION OF
SOME NATURAL FERTILIZER MATERIALS

Material	Nitrogen (N)	Phosphoric Acid (P)	Potash (K)
BULKY ORGANIC MATERIALS			
Alfalfa hay	2.5	.5	2.0
Bean straw	1.2	.3	1.2
Crabgrass	.66	.19	.71
Grain straw	.6	.2	1.0
Oak leaves	.80	.35	.15
Peanut hulls	1.5	—	.8
Peat	2.3	.4	.8
Sawdust	.2	—	.2
Seaweed (kelp)	.6	—	1.3
Timothy hay	1.0	.2	1.5
Winery pomaces	1.5	1.5	.8
MANURES			
Bat guano	10.0	4.5	2.0
Cow manure, dried	1.3	.9	.8
Cow manure, fresh	.5	.2	.5
Hen manure, dried, with litter	2.8	2.8	1.5
Hen manure, fresh	1.1	.9	.5
Horse manure, fresh	.6	.3	.5
Pig manure, fresh	.6	.5	.4
Sheep manure, dried	1.4	1.0	3.0
Sheep manure, fresh	.9	.5	.8

Material	Nitrogen (N)	Phosphoric Acid (P)	Potash (K)
Rock Powders			
Basic slag	—	8.0–17.0	—
Greensand (glauconite)	—	1.4	4.0–9.5
Hybro-tite	—	.002	—
Rock phosphate (apatite)	—	38.0–40.0	4.5
Vegetative and Animal Materials			
Bonemeal, steamed	2.0	22.0	—
Castor pomace	6.0	1.9	.5
Cocoa shell meal	2.5	1.5	2.5
Cottonseed meal	6.0	3.0	1.0
Dried blood meal	13.0	1.5	.8
Feathers	15.0	30.0	—
Fish meal	10.0	6.0	—
Fish scrap	5.0	3.0	—
Garbage tankage	1.5	2.0	.7
Hoof and horn meal	12.0	2.0	—
Soybean meal	7.0	1.2	1.5
Tankage, animal	9.0	6.0	—
Tankage, processed	7.0	1.0	.1
Tobacco dust and stems	1.5	.5	5.0
Wood ashes	—	1.8	5.0

NPK

NPK, as you probably know, describes the content of the major nutrients necessary for plant life and growth: nitrogen, phosphorus, and potassium (K). The numbers on a package of commercial fertilizer tell you the NPK content of the fertilizer. For example, 10-6-4 means that the fertilizer contains 10 percent nitrogen, 6 percent phosphorus, and 4 percent potassium. Fertilizers with NPK numbers of 10-6-4 or 20-10-5 are called "complete" because they contain a percentage of all three major nutrients. Superphosphate (0-20-0), on the other hand, is "incomplete" because it only contains a percentage of phosphorus and no significant percentage of either nitrogen or potassium.

Nitrogen

It may seem that we have belabored the various ways of getting nitrogen into your compost pile. But never underestimate the importance of nitrogen. It is perhaps the most important nutrient of all, mainly because plants themselves contain so much of it. It gives them their healthy dark green color and is essential for leaf and stem growth. You will easily recognize a plant with nitrogen deficiency by its sickly yellow coloring. The problem with nitrogen is that it is so mobile. That means that it escapes from compost or soil very easily, either in the form of gas or by being washed away. One of the most important reasons for composting at all is to restore nitrogen to the soil, so obviously you should be making as much effort as possible to store up nitrogen in your compost pile.

Phosphorus

Phosphorus stimulates growth, flowering, and root development. Cell division is vital to plant growth, and it would be impossible without the presence of phosphorus. Plants without phosphorus grow slowly (if at all), look droopy, and have weak root systems. But phosphorus, unlike nitrogen, is immobile. It tends to stay for a long time wherever it is applied. It does not leach and is not given off as a gas.

The best sources of phosphorus are rock phosphate and bone meal. (Bone meal also contains nitrogen.) Superphosphate is rock phosphate that has been treated with sulfuric acid to make it more soluble. Unfortunately, in the treatment process many of the valuable minor elements of phosphate rock, such as boron, zinc, nickel, and iodine, have been lost. Phosphate rock is often added to the compost pile in a light sprinkling every several layers.

Potassium

Potassium (potash) is necessary for the development of chlorophyll, that almost magical substance in green plants that makes the miracle of photosynthesis possible. Potassium also strengthens plant tissue and makes plants more disease resistant. Plants that receive too little potassium look stunted. Potassium washes out of compost quite easily, but it can never escape as a gas. You can restore it to the heap or the garden by adding wood ashes, greensand, or muriate of potash.

Many composter-gardeners worry too much about producing compost with a very high and well-balanced NPK. Would it be terribly disillusioning to be told that compost is not a miracle fertilizer? In most good compost, the content of NPK is actually very low. In fact, it usually does not have a high enough percentage of NPK to be considered a fertilizer at all. But you can boost the NPK by adding natural sources of nitrogen, phosphorus, and potassium to your compost pile. Or worry about nutrients later on and add fertilizer when you mix compost into your soil.

Element	Symbol	Function in Plant	Deficiency Symptoms	Excess Symptoms
Nitrogen	N	Gives dark green color to plant. Increases growth of leaf and stem. Influences crispness and quality of leaf crops. Stimulates rapid early growth.	Light green to yellow leaves. Stunted growth.	Dark green. Excessive growth. Retarded maturity. Loss of buds or fruit.
Phosphorus	P	Stimulates early formation and growth of roots. Gives plants a rapid and vigorous start. Is important in formation of seed. Gives hardiness to fall-seeded grasses and grains.	Red or purple leaves. Cell division retardation.	Possible tie-up of other essential elements.
Potassium	K	Increases vigor of plants and resistance to disease. Stimulates production of strong, stiff stalks. Promotes production of sugar, starches, oils. Increases plumpness of grains and seed. Improves quality of crop yield.	Reduced vigor. Susceptibility to diseases. Thin skin and small fruit.	Coarse, poor-colored fruit. Reduced absorption of magnesium and calcium.

Heat

I have already mentioned the practice of using temperature as a factor in helping you determine when to turn the pile. Some gardeners are reluctant to turn their heaps because they are afraid they will lose a lot of heat. They are right, of course. But the pile will regenerate heat again very quickly, sometimes in a matter of two to twelve hours. In other words, turning interrupts the heat fermentation process only briefly.

Composters seem to worry about heating more than anything else. A friend of mine, a new gardener, came out of his door one chilly morning and was horrified to discover steamy vapor rising out of the ventilating holes in his pile. He nervously mentioned it to several of us over lunch. When he was finally assured that vapor was no cause for alarm and that it was, in fact, reason to cheer, others in the group immediately began to express concern that their piles did not give off a lot of steam.

Generally, I think we have placed too much emphasis and value on home compost pile temperatures that are as high as 150° to 160°F. Sanitation in massive public compost systems is one thing, but it is not necessarily true that higher temperatures mean faster decomposition. Thermophilic composting does have the advantage of killing pathogenic organisms and weed seeds. Mesophiles do not perform this function, but these midtemperature bacteria are every bit as effective "rotters" as thermophiles. If you don't use plant refuse, hay, or straw

that has gone to seed, and if you don't use diseased matter, you should not have to worry about intense heating all that much.

You want some heat. Psychrophiles will be at work even at very low temperatures, but for decomposition to be at all effective the temperature of the pile must be above 55°F. On the other hand, heating can be tricky if it gets out of control. Earthworms are killed at 130°F, and they will not stick around and endanger themselves for very long in temperatures that even approach that figure. Azobacteria, the precious microorganisms that transform nitrogen gas into a form that plants can use, are killed at temperatures above 160°F. Excessive heat is far more dangerous than no heat at all. So try to establish some sort of happy medium as far as heat is concerned, and if the temperature goes above 150°F, disassemble the pile to cool it down.

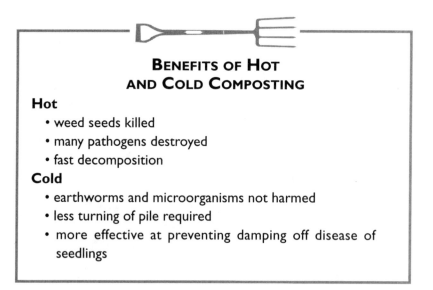

BENEFITS OF HOT AND COLD COMPOSTING

Hot
- weed seeds killed
- many pathogens destroyed
- fast decomposition

Cold
- earthworms and microorganisms not harmed
- less turning of pile required
- more effective at preventing damping off disease of seedlings

A pile that is too small may give off a lot of its heat to the surrounding atmosphere. This may account for its apparent lack of heating. But the inability to accumulate enough materials for a big pile should not be an excuse for not composting at all. Do not be discouraged and start thinking that you cannot make good compost because a lot of heat does not build up in your pile. If your pile is activated with soil, for instance, don't expect it to heat up as much as a neighboring one that is activated with manure.

Compost piles work most efficiently in the summer months because the surrounding air is warmer and slower during the rest of the year. In fall, winter, and early spring, the heating-up process can be enhanced and the pile made to function longer if you insulate it and add lots of high-nitrogen materials like leguminous plants and animal matter. However, by doing this you lower the carbon/nitrogen ratio and will sacrifice some nitrogen in exchange for this heat.

You need no fancy and costly devices to gauge and record the temperature near the middle of the pile. You can buy a composting thermometer or you can stick a piece of metal pipe into the pile and leave it there for a few minutes. If it feels hot or warm when you pull it out, all is probably well.

Use a compost thermo-meter or metal pipe to gauge the temperature of the compost.

Pathogens

When you add compost to your soil, you can unwittingly spread disease if you're not careful. Disease-causing microbes can get into your compost pile by catching a free ride on any of the materials you add to your pile. You want these pathogens to be killed off during the composting process so your future plantings aren't infected by the addition of compost to your soil. In an active pile, the pathogens are up against some heavy competition for food from the beneficial bacteria. The beneficial bacteria also produce organic compounds that actually inhibit growth of disease-causing bacteria. (You and I know these compounds as antibiotics.) And, if the beneficial bacteria are working hard, they heat up the pile to around 140°F, and the heat kills the pathogens. So ideally, pathogens aren't a problem. But let's face it, we live in a less-than-perfect world, and maybe conditions in your pile are less than ideal. If you don't think your pile will reach 130°F, play it safe and avoid adding any diseased vegetable or flower plant, or anything else that appears unhealthy, to your compost heap.

A WORD OF CAUTION

People with weakened immune systems should avoid handling manure and undecomposed compost. The bacteria and fungal spores could present a risk to their health. Fully decomposed compost, on the other hand, can be handled. Wearing gloves is a good precaution for everyone.

Insects

Insects in your pile are a good sign: They help break down the organic matter. One notable exception is symphylans, or symphilids, which resemble centipedes. They have a hearty appetite for rotting organic matter and tender emerging root tips. They seem to be more of a problem in certain parts of the country (the Northwest, for example), and in these locations some people limit the amount of compost they use to reduce the likelihood of introducing symphylans at the same time.

Maggots (fly larvae) can be an annoyance in some piles, since flies like to breed in damp hay or straw. This is why some people will lay screening over the insulative layer to keep the parent flies out. Others will cap a pile with a layer of sod or loose soil, which deters flies. Adding soil is also supposed to trap beneficial gases, like nitrogen, which might be escaping from the pile. On the negative side, soil on top allows weeds to establish themselves.

Weeds

You will be amazed at how fast weeds can grow in your compost. Don't let them ambush the pile's water supply. Weed roots that grow close to the surface of the pile will intercept moisture before it has a chance to get to the material below. This past spring, a pole bean seed somehow found its way into my compost pile when I was planting seeds one Saturday. Within a couple of days — and this is no exaggeration — there, growing out of the pile, was a 12-inch-high stem with tiny bean leaves at the top. As soon as I saw it, I dashed into the house, all set to write a wonderful children's story called "Jack and the Beanstalk." My wife threw cold water on the whole thing by calmly reminding me that I was too late for that one. I have since found, after reading Sam Ogden's *Step-by-Step to Organic Vegetable Growing*, that I am actually not the first to think that the original inspiration for that fairy tale might have been a lowly compost pile and a pole bean seed.

The moral of my story: To avoid trouble with a giant or with an overly dry compost pile, pull out the weeds before they get too big, turn the roots toward the sun, and leave them on the pile to die.

TROUBLE-SHOOTING CHART

Problem	Possible Cause	Solution
Unpleasant odor from pile	Not enough oxygen due to compaction	Aerate
	Not enough oxygen due to overwatering	Add carbon materials such as cornstalks, leaves, or wood chips to soak up excess water; improve aeration
	If odor of ammonia, too much nitrogen	Add carbon materials and aerate
Pile not heating up	Lack of nitrogen	Mix in a nitrogen source such as fresh grass clippings, fresh manure, or blood meal. If you can't mix the materials easily, try making holes in the pile and pouring in the nitrogen materials
	Not enough moisture	Stick a garden hose down into the pile in several locations and water; or poke holes into the pile with a rod and pour water down the holes using a watering can
	Pile needs to be turned	Use a pitchfork to bring materials from the outside of the pile into the center
	Compost may be finished; if it looks dark and crumbly and smells earthy instead of moldy or rotten, it's probably ready	
Compost is damp and warm only in the center	Pile is too small	Gather more materials and rebuild a larger pile
Nothing is happening	You were daydreaming while reading this book	Read the book again!

We'd love your thoughts...

Your reactions, criticisms, things you did or didn't like about this Storey Book. Please use space below (or write a letter if you'd prefer — even send photos!) telling how you've made use of the information . . . how you've put it to work . . . the more details the better! Thanks in advance for your help in building our library of good Storey Books.

Pamela B. Art

Publisher

Book Title: _____

Purchased From: _____

Comments: _____

_____

_____

_____

_____

_____

Your Name: _____

Address: _____

☐ Please check here if you'd like our latest Storey's *Books for Country Living* Catalog.

☐ You have my permission to quote from my comments, and use these quotations in ads, brochures, mail, and other promotions used to market your books.

Signed _____ Date _____

From: _____

BUSINESS REPLY MAIL

FIRST-CLASS MAIL   PERMIT NO 2   POWNAL, VT

POSTAGE WILL BE PAID BY ADDRESSEE

STOREY'S BOOKS FOR COUNTRY LIVING

STOREY COMMUNICATIONS INC

RR 1   BOX 105

POWNAL VT 05261-9988

In reference to the ever-frustrating observation that "nothing is happening," remember the following: Even after reading all the compost advice you can get your hands on, until you've built a few compost piles you may feel like my daughter did not so long ago. She expressed an interest in reading. Delighted, my wife and I spent several days teaching her to recite the twenty-six letters of the alphabet — the very rudiments of written language. When she finally had learned it all, she said, "Yes, but how do I read?"

The End Product
and How to Use It

All right, finally, the inevitable question: "How do we know when compost is done, and how long does it take?" I will have to admit, right off the bat, that the second part of this question is probably more difficult to answer than the first. In a way, asking how long it takes to make compost is like wanting to know the exact date of the last killing frost in the spring. Clearly, these are two of life's little unpredictables.

Because there are so many "ifs" involved, there can only be some general guidelines as far as any sort of a composting timetable is concerned. We have already seen that if you have the right equipment, such as a shredder, fourteen-day compost can be made by using the University of California method. If, on the other hand, you have more time, it may be better to wait longer for your compost. Perhaps you generate enough waste around your home to have several compost piles going at once and can afford to let fermentation go on for two years or more the way Samuel Ogden does.

CHARACTERISTICS OF IDEAL "FINISHED" COMPOST

- It should be free of nearly all pathogenic organisms and weed seeds.
- It should have an adequate supply of at least some of the major nutrients, and should contain a variety of minor nutrients. The ideal final product will show traces of manganese, boron, sodium, zinc, and other elements. If you had enough compost to spread over your entire garden each year, you should, in a fairly short time, be able to correct magnesium, copper, iron, and boron deficiencies in the soil. This does not mean, you will remember, that in all cases compost is a complete fertilizer that needs no further supplements.
- Finished compost should be crumbly. "Crumbly" is another one of those vague terms like "well-rotted manure," "friable soil," and "tilth" that gardeners like to use. It means sort of fluffy, not stringy. Tough, highly carbonaceous things like straw fibers, for example, may still be intact. But if the compost is ready for use, you should be able to crush and pulverize material like this between your fingertips. Crumbly compost, like crumbly soil, allows air to penetrate and holds moisture well, but allows excess water to drain away.
- Finished compost is dark in color. Like earthworm castings, good compost has been called "black gold." If it is *truly* black — rather than deep brown — and has a greasy texture, it may also be called "black butter." Black butter is usually the product of a too-moist anaerobic compost system and is less desirable than the aerobically produced stuff.
- Though it may not look like earth, good finished compost should *smell* sweet and earthy — never moldy and rotten.
- It will have undergone a drop in temperature from somewhere near 150°F to whatever the temperature is outside the compost pile. Compost that is still much warmer than the surrounding air needs more decomposition time.
- It should still consist of at least 25 to 30 percent organic matter. In this sense it is even more valuable than actual manure.

Four to six months seems to be the normal amount of time needed to make superior compost here in the northeastern United States. If we were to start a pile in November, it would take somewhat longer than that. If we were to start one in June, if we attended to it faithfully, and if we turned it carefully and regularly, it might take less time than that. If you live in a climate that is warmer than ours, closer to that of Indore, India, you can probably do a satisfactory job of composting most kinds of organic matter in the three months that Sir Albert Howard recommends.

The safest bet is to think in terms of giving the compost a chance to decompose for a little *longer* than seems necessary.

Spreading in the Fall

The most advantageous time to incorporate large volumes of compost into the garden is in the fall. Spread whatever compost you have been making over the summer over the entire growing area. You can do this any time after the first killing frost and before the soil becomes frozen hard. It is not a requirement that it be turned or tilled right into the garden; it will do the soil a lot of good if you just let it lie there over the winter. If you do have the right equipment (a rototiller or a small garden tractor with a harrow), or if you are an ambitious soul when it comes to spading by hand, you will be doing your garden even more good if you mix the compost in with the soil

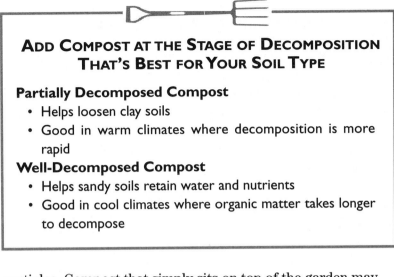

particles. Compost that simply sits on top of the garden may dry out quickly, and some of the nutrients it contains may escape into the atmosphere as gas.

Storage Problems

This brings to mind the problem of compost storage. It is hard to "put compost by" effectively. A pile of rich, rotted organic matter will keep *for a while* if it is covered with plastic or a canvas tarp to discourage leaching. As a general rule, however, it would be better to add compost into the garden too early, perhaps before it is fully "completed," rather than too late. If allowed to sit around for too long after it is finished, it may lose much of its value. The further the materials are allowed to decompose — without the addition of some fresh, fibrous organic matter — the more colloidal the compost becomes as it breaks down into smaller and smaller pieces. This in itself is not necessarily bad. The problem is that it is difficult for air to penetrate any great distance through such a fine aggregate, and anaerobia may be the result. Don't leave a pile of finished compost unused for more than half a year or so at the most.

Spreading in the Spring

If you happen to have a batch of compost that is ripening in the spring, and if it appears that you are not going to be adding further material as the summer progresses, there is no need to wait until fall before you use it. Finished or nearly finished compost is fairly effective if it is used about a month before planting time in the spring. It can be broadcast and worked into the soil at that time. Besides offering fertilizer to the garden and conditioning the soil, the compost will have even more value because it retains heat from the sun much better than most ordinary garden soil.

Some have been concerned that adding compost in the springtime will rob nitrogen from soil as the compost continues to decompose. I have never found this to be the case with compost, although I have never taken any accurate measurements of the C/N in soil before and after compost was added to it. Even so, it seems safe to assume that the C/N of even partially rotted, "unstable" compost should be low enough so that no nitrogen should have to be borrowed from the surrounding earth. If you add large quantities of partially decomposed compost, you might want to do a soil test after mixing it in, and add nitrogen if needed. (Nitrogen supplement *is usually* necessary, however, if you till in a lot of *un*composted hay or straw, which has a high carbon content.)

I would recommend adding *finished* compost to your soil or using compost as a mulch anytime — especially in the hottest, driest periods of midsummer. You should never have to worry about nitrogen deficiency in garden plants if you do.

Compost for Planting

All your plants can benefit from compost — from seedlings to potted plants to garden crops to shrubs and trees. The applications vary slightly, so I'll mention some ways you can use compost with different crops. Keep in mind that these are only a few suggestions, and here again, be creative and experiment to find out what works best in your gardens.

All your plants can benefit from compost.

Don't spread and turn under your entire supply of compost all at once. Save a little to use with some of your plantings. Because compost does not contain everything plants need for their nutrition, it is not a good idea to plant most vegetables in pure compost alone. I doubt very much, as a matter of fact, that the pole bean sprout that got started in my compost pile could have continued its frightening rate of growth.

I am told that right after germination is the time when very young plants are most likely to suffer from undernourishment. The seedlings have not had time to send out a very extensive root system at that point. Pure loam, or even a combination of loam and compost, is likely to lack some nutrients — particularly phosphorus. A soil test will tell you what nutrients are needed.

But be careful. Try to plan far enough ahead so that fertilizing can be done well in advance of whenever your seeds are to be planted. This will give the particles of fertilizer time to dissolve in the damp compost and give the chemicals time to work their way in among the particles of organic matter. Be sure that you use no more than half of the fertilizer you might normally use to side-dress a particular plant or spread over a certain area of garden space, or you risk burning the seedlings.

I have found that compost to which no fertilizer has been added will never burn seeds, even if seeds are sown directly on top of it. The same is true of "inoculated" compost, if the fertilizer has been added well beforehand.

General Soil Improvement

Compost can be incorporated into your garden soil before planting, just like you would use other soil amendments such as peat moss or manure. In general, 5 to 10 percent organic matter is optimal for healthy plant growth. You can have your soil tested to find out its percentage of organic matter so you'll know how much compost to add. Not all labs that perform soil tests have the capability to test for organic matter content.

If you have a strong back for double-digging, you can dig a trench and lay compost 3 to 4 inches deep in the bottom before adding the topsoil back in. If you use a tiller, you can spread a 1-inch layer of compost on the surface of your soil and till it in. If you practice no-till gardening and don't wish to disturb the soil, you can spread compost on the soil surface as a mulch. More on mulching in a minute.

If you're starting with a new garden area and need more topsoil, you can make it with compost. Simply layer compost 3 inches deep on top of the ground and till it in 5 to 6 inches deep. Do this for three or four years in a row and voilà, topsoil!

To double-dig, remove a row of soil one spade wide and one spade deep, then dig an adjacent row of the same dimensions and place its soil in the first row. Continue all the way down the bed, and fill in the final row with the soil from the first row. Compost can be added into the bottom of each row before topsoil is replaced.

Annual Flowers and Vegetables

As part of routine maintenance of garden beds, mix
2 inches of compost into soil to a depth of 6 to 8 inches.
Screen it through a ½-inch sieve before adding it to
your soil. This will remove the large pieces of
undecomposed material that you can then
throw back into your compost pile.

*Add compost as a side-dressing to
give plantings a boost throughout
the season*

Tomatoes. When I get ready to transplant tomatoes in the
garden proper, I dig a furrow anywhere from 4 to 6 inches deep
and fill it about half full of rich garbage compost. I water-soak
the compost-soil-sand mixture in the milk carton or seed flats
and remove the young plant — trying to keep the soil surrounding its roots as intact as possible. I remove all but the uppermost
leaves on the plant and lay the roots and long stem down in the
furrow on top of the compost. I cover them with soil, leaving
only the few remaining leaves sticking out of the ground. The
stem, fed by the rich compost, will start to grow tiny root hairs
almost immediately, and within a couple of weeks the stem will
have transformed itself into a long and complicated tangle of
roots. This makes a very strong foundation from which the rest
of the plants can grow healthy and well nourished.

Peppers. Peppers are usually planted in the same row,
interspaced with the tomatoes as companion plants. They are
set upright on the compost, not lying down.

Beans. When I plant pole beans in my own garden, I
follow a procedure much like the method described by Sam
Ogden in *Step-by-Step to Organic Vegetable Growing*. I dig a

row of holes about 3 feet apart, 8 inches deep, and 2 feet in diameter. Then, with a crowbar, I poke a much deeper and smaller hole and set the bean pole — a straight stick 7 or 8 feet long cut from the woods near home — in the center of the larger hole.

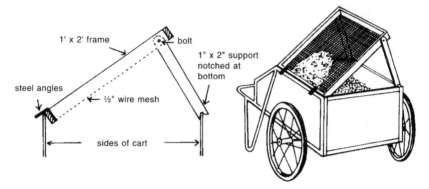

This handy device serves as both a compost cart and a sieve.

I fill the bigger hole with a compost and fertilizer mixture and lay a circle of seeds right on top of the compost. Each seed is about 8 inches away from the pole. A ninth seed is set in the middle of the circle, right next to the pole — mostly for good luck. About an inch of loose soil is put over the top of the seeds and tamped down by hand. Early plantings of Romano or Kentucky Wonder beans seem to germinate more quickly in compost than those planted in regular soil. The roots of the young plants have no difficulty finding their way down into the loose organic matter and are able to draw goodness from it right away. Soon the leaves are very large and dark green, and, in time, the beans superb.

I sometimes use the same technique when I plant hills of corn, cucumbers, or squash — leaving out the pole, naturally. Peas, beans of all kinds, grapes, lettuce, cabbage, cauliflower, broccoli, raspberries, Brussels sprouts, chard, spinach, and other greens can be planted with compost, too. It takes just a bit longer than planting or transplanting the conventional way. It is simply a matter of making a shallow trench or hole with a

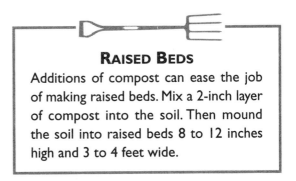

RAISED BEDS

Additions of compost can ease the job of making raised beds. Mix a 2-inch layer of compost into the soil. Then mound the soil into raised beds 8 to 12 inches high and 3 to 4 feet wide.

hoe, shovel, or furrower putting compost in the depression laying the seeds on the compost covering them and firming the soil.

Perennials

Perennials, like asparagus and rhubarb, will do well if their roots are planted on top of a trench 8 inches wide and 1½ feet deep ,which has been filled with fertilized compost.

To add compost to perennials that are already planted, gently mix a 1- to 2-inch layer into the topsoil or apply it on top as a mulch. If you try to work compost deeply into the soil, you may damage tender roots.

Shrubs and Trees

Spread 1 to 2 inches of compost around plants and work it gently into the surface of the soil. Then cover with a mulch of cocoa hulls or bark chips. Acid-loving plants such as rhododen-drons will love an acid compost, which you can make by using oak or beech leaves, sawdust, and pine needles.

DID YOU KNOW?

While nurseries used to recommend mixing compost into the planting holes, now they usually advise against mixing in amendments. Plants tend to restrict their root systems to the small amended area instead of spreading them out into the surrounding soil.

Small Fruits

To plant strawberries, you might build a little mound of compost in the bottom of a shallow furrow and drape the roots of the young plants over the mound so they cover it like a skirt. Then bring the soil up to the plant just below the crown.

BioSelector

This BioSelector provides recommendations for cultural practices and compost applications based on the percentage of organic matter in your soil.

Organic Matter (O.M.) Test Result	Possible Problems
Below 2% O.M., LOW	Low microbe and earthworm activity. Nitrogen deficiencies likely. Poor nutrient exchange and low water-holding capacity. Garden crops will not survive stress.
2% to 3.5% O.M., MEDIUM	Microbe and earthworm activity better, but still low. Nitrogen may still be deficient. Soil's ability to hold nutrients and moisture is still not adequate to avoid plant stress.
3.5% to 5% O.M., GOOD	Tilth, structure, and water-holding should be adequate. Healthy, productive crops are more likely.
Above 5% O.M., EXCELLENT	High soil life is providing efficient nutrient exchange. Moisture-holding capacity should be good, regardless of weather stress.

Grapes and berries can benefit from a 3-inch layer of compost mulch in early spring. The mulch will act as a weed barrier and also feed the plants.

Remedies	Recommended Finished Compost Applications per 1000 Square Feet
Increase organic matter level over next 2 to 3 years. Use foliar nutrients and side-dress plants. Grow green manures. Apply composts and mulches. Rotate vegetables as much as possible and sow cover crops.	2000 lbs. (approximately 2 cu. yds.) This represents a ¼" to ⅓" thick layer, which should then be thoroughly mixed into top 6 inches.
Foliar nutrients are still recommended in addition to composts. Continue to grow green manure. Mulch and sow cover crops where possible. Organic mineral fertilizers still needed, broadcast in the row. Side-dress heavy feeders.	1000 lbs. (approximately 1 cu. yd.) This represents about a ⅛" layer. Incorporate into top 6 inches.
Continue growing green manures and applying composts. Heavy feeder crops still need fertilization.	500 lbs. Thoroughly mix into top 4 inches.
Apply only maintenance amounts of organic matter. Too much raw matter could overload the soil ecosystem and tie up trace minerals. Green manuring should maintain organic levels except in the Deep South.	200 lbs. Thoroughly mix into top 4 inches.

Adapted from Necessary Trading Company's BioSelector™ chart.
© 1987 Necessary Trading Company, New Castle, Virginia.

Fruit Trees

Your trees will benefit from compost applied in a circular band around each tree, starting 2 to 3 feet away from the trunk and extending to the drip line at the ends of the branches. First work any grass into the soil then apply compost. If you've got the time for annual applications, use ½ to 1 inch of compost and work it into the upper 2 inches of soil. Or add a 3- to 4-inch layer of compost, which will last as many years. Cover the compost with a mulch of old hay or grass clippings.

You can also make compost right under the tree so the tree roots can take advantage of the finished compost and nutrients that leach from the pile. Build your pile in a band or ring about 2 feet high and 3 feet from the trunk.

Apply a side-dressing of compost out to the drip line of deciduous trees.

Garden Mulch

Screened compost makes a handy mulch around closely spaced vegetable and flower plants because it doesn't damage the stems. If you have an abundance of compost, you can afford to be generous with it as a mulch. But if you never have enough you'll get the most benefit out of mixing it into your soil.

You probably know all about manure tea and what a magical elixir it is for your plants. Compost tea also gives your plants a good dose of nutrients. Mix one part compost with 5 parts water, stir several times, and let it sit for several days. Use the tea to water new transplants and houseplants and to spray on young seedlings. You can use the same batch of compost to make several batches of tea.

You can make compost tea in a clean 55-gallon drum by filling one-fourth of the drum with compost and filling the rest with water. Stir this brew every once in a while when you are strolling past the drum and happen to think of it. After a couple of months, dip a bucket or watering can into the drum when you want strong compost tea.

A friend of mine in Stowe, Vermont, has developed a slightly more sophisticated way of making the same stuff — without stirring. He also uses a doctored-up 55-gallon oil drum, which is set on cinder blocks. He puts some compost into a burlap bag, ties off the top of the bag with twine, puts the bag in the drum (which is already filled with water), and fastens the twine to a hook that is welded to the outside of the drum near the top.

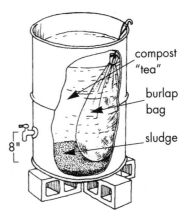

compost "tea"

burlap bag

sludge

8"

About 8 inches from the *bottom* of the drum there is an old faucet that has also been welded into the side of the steel container. Through this he can draw off compost water as he needs it. My friend points out that it is important that the faucet not be placed any lower than 6 to 8 inches from the bottom of the barrel. "Sludge" from the big burlap tea bag will settle to the bottom of the barrel, making a bed of residue 4 to 6 inches deep; this can clog the faucet. These dregs need to be cleaned out every three years or so, and they make wonderful fertilizer. He uses it on the garden, while his wife applies the compost tea to houseplants and seedlings with a kitchen baster.

Seedlings

You can make a seedling mixture of one-third screened compost, one-third soil, and one-third coarse sand, perlite, or vermiculite. This medium will supply your young plants with all the nutrients they need until transplanting at six to eight weeks. The compost provides a slow release of nutrients as opposed to inorganic fertilizers that can burn seedlings initially and then cause nutrient deficiency all in a matter of weeks.

COMPOST AND DISEASE SUPPRESSION

Compost has the ability to suppress plant diseases such as damping off, powdery and downy mildews, and late blight of potato. Several researchers have found that certain composts activate disease resistance in plants. In addition, the beneficial microorganisms keep plant disease pathogens inactive.

Tea made from manure-containing compost can be sprayed on plants to coat the foliage with microbes that suppress disease. Teas provide immediate short-term protection; compost acts slowly over a longer period.

Potted Plants

Compost can also be used to make potting soil for indoor plants. Strain it first to remove clumps and debris, then mix about one-third compost and two-thirds soil and it's ready for planting. If your plants are in pots, add an inch of compost as a mulch and your plants will get nutrients every time you water.

Lawns

Well-decomposed compost can be incorporated in the soil when planting a new lawn. Spread a 2-inch layer over the area and till it in before seeding. An established lawn will benefit from a top dressing of finely screened compost. Apply it in spring or fall after aerating your lawn.

TOO MUCH COMPOST?

The question is sometimes raised: Is it possible to get *too much* organic matter into the soil? The answer is yes. Here are some concerns:

1. If all of the organic matter you use is all of one kind and is highly carbonaceous, you could throw the C/N ratio so far out of balance that the soil might have a hard time growing much of anything.

2. Soil pH also can be affected by too much compost. If you saturate a given piece of land with some sort of highly acidic organic material, you might seriously influence that soil's pH for a while. You might also want to add lime to your soil when you add the compost. Check the pH of your soil with and without compost so you'll know what effect your compost is having.

3. I've heard gardeners complain of garden beds drying out too quickly after the addition of too much compost. Incompletely broken down compost can be *hydrophobic* — that is, it repels water just like peat moss does before it's completely saturated. This usually isn't a problem because the compost will continue to break down in the soil, and in a month or so this tendency will disappear. But sawdust-based compost can cause an ongoing problem with water repellency because sawdust is slow to decompose and it is hydrophobic to begin with.

4. If you live in a fairly dry climate and want to be on the safe side, be sure your compost is well decomposed before adding it to your garden and keep the sawdust to a minimum. It can also reduce the efficiency of soaker hoses because the water repellency characteristics and the large pore spaces of incompletely decomposed compost can interfere with the capillary action that helps move water slowly through the soil. If you notice problems once the compost is added to your garden, just incorporate more topsoil.

How much compost is too much? That's debatable, and it depends on the makeup of your compost, your climate, and what kind of soil you have. But the general recommendation is that your soil should contain anywhere from 5 to 10 percent organic matter.

A Composting Experiment

One year, a group of our neighbors who owned a tennis court collectively decided that they should turn their clay court — too wet to play on too much of the time — into a hard-surface, all-weather court. The contractor dug up the old clay and asked permission to deposit it in a clearing among some trees not far from us. We agreed. He spread it around carefully, so as not to harm the roots of any of the trees, and smoothed it with a bulldozer. By the time he finished, the little clearing seemed such an attractive garden spot that we decided to see if we could eventually grow something there to reinforce what our small gardens at home produced.

This decision was made with only moderate enthusiasm because we knew that the soil the contractor had put there was the stickiest kind of clay — totally devoid, as far as we could see, of any sort of organic matter. To make matters worse, a simple pH test revealed that it was quite alkaline, possibly the result of some lime-based "hardener" that may have been put on the court or of some other chemicals designed to keep down the dust during the dry summer days. All signs seemed to indicate that this place in the woods

Preparing the soil

was going to be a desert — for a few years at least — unless we took some sort of drastic steps to improve the soil. Initial long-range plans called for a multiyear program of green manuring — buckwheat in summer, ryegrass in the fall — to build up the earthworm, microbe, and organic matter content.

After a few days of dry late-May weather, the old tennis court material changed from gluey mud, which accumulated on my shoe sole after three steps, to concretelike hardpan where I could leave no tracks. I spent one whole evening turning it up with our powerful tiller, thinking that I was getting it ready for a planting of buckwheat. The tiller and I did such a nice job of loosening the tough clay that the old court again began to take on the look of a potential garden. It looked so much that way that my wife asked optimistically, "Say, what would happen if we planted some vegetables here this year?"

Why not? In the cold light of dawn things looked less promising, but we forged ahead by making furrows with some second-rate compost we had made at home from leaves and spoiled hay. By midmorning the noise of our labor had attracted a crowd of neighbors and we put everyone to work. Suddenly we had a community garden. Together we planted corn, lettuce, several kinds of chard, beets, soybeans, Chinese cabbage, cucumbers, peas, bush beans, radishes, and squash. The seeds were laid on top of the rotted organic matter, the rows covered with loose soil and carefully walked upon by many children's sneakers. Then a small amount of 16-10-20 fertilizer was sprinkled over the top of each row. It turned out to be a rather festive Saturday morning. Even so, no one really held high hopes for the success of the garden.

Planting the garden

Less than a week later, after a rain shower or two, radishes that had been planted along with other seeds to mark the rows were up and going strong. And a week after that nearly everything else we planted had put in an appearance, too. To our surprise and delight, the seed germination must have been close to 100 percent. It was so complete that plantings made too close together by some of the kids had to be thinned.

The beginnings of our garden

By now we are growing such a fine crop of vegetables that some of the people in the neighborhood dread the possibility of being slaves to freezer bags, pressure cookers, and canning jars during the months of August and September. Our little desert clearing is bearing fruit, and with tongue in cheek everyone is suddenly blaming me for all of the work I have provided.

The reward of our labor — an abundant harvest

Now each one of us is going to have to cultivate and weed another garden besides our own, and we may fight about who harvests what. We are going to have to collect leaves in the fall, sheet-compost them, and plant winter rye. If local bands of raccoons and squirrels are able to do what the woodchucks and rabbits have failed to do so far — cover our secret plot in the woods — they may feast on our ripened corn. If they do, and I fear they will, we will probably have to build a fence for next year.

Such are the dubious rewards of success, however ill-planned. A headache, sometimes, this self-sufficient living. A lot of work, too. Satisfying though. Satisfying, indeed. And I can't help but wonder if this minor first-year triumph with an old tennis court would really have been possible without the compost . . . .

The Times, They Are A-Changin'

Twenty years ago, composting was a little-practiced art (or is it a science?), and we were merrily carting valuable organic stuff to the dump. There were but a handful of public composting projects and very few private composting operations. Now dumps are called landfills, and more and more of them are banning yard trash. The number of residential yard waste composting sites has jumped from 651 in 1988 to over 3,000.

Just in case composting and recycling render the landfill obsolete, there is a place you can go in the future to have a good look at our trashy past. The Hackensack, New Jersey, Meadowlands Development Commission operates a museum devoted to trash. It's appropriately located in the Meadowlands, where garbage has been dumped for more than half a century. The museum gives visitors a sense of being inside a landfill, walking through mountains of trash. Interactive exhibits, including a wall-sized vertical board game called "Composting — A Great Cleanup Game," attract over 40,000 visitors a year.

All of this is good news. It means things are changing. Not only are we making something useful out of the tons of materials we used to throw away, we are taking better care of Mother Earth by nourishing the soil — one backyard and one community at a time. In the process, we are beginning to appreciate nature's cycles and the abundance of life in our soil. We can almost hear the munching of insects. We are learning to admire simple earthly things like the granular droppings of friendly earthworms. We are beginning to hail the passing armies of bacteria, seeing them as allies rather than dirty germs. We are getting to know fungi as healthy things and are realizing that rotting is as consistent with growing as sowing is with harvesting.

We are becoming more and more aware of ourselves, too — more conscious of each other and of the entire natural and cultural milieu in which we live. We are starting to understand that the problems we face as individuals extend to all corners of the earth.

If it is not magnifying the importance of composting too much to say it, making compost enriches our lives almost as much as it does our gardens. It seems to harmonize our being here with the way the world ought to be. Composting can make you feel good about yourself. If you don't already know it, you'll see.

Sources

Composting Supplies

Alsto's Handy Helpers
P.O. Box 1267
Galesberg, IL 61401
Phone: 309-347-2010

Brookstone Company
5 Vose Farm Road
Peterborough, NH 03458
Fax: 603-924-7181

W. Atlee Burpee & Company
300 Park Avenue
Warminster, PA 18974
Phone: 800-888-1447
Fax: 800-487-5530
http://garden.burpee.com/
index.html

Earl May Seed & Nursery
208 N. Elm Street
Shenandoah, IA 51603
Phone: 800-831-4193

Gardener's Eden
P.O. Box 7307
San Francisco, CA 94120-7307
Phone:800-822-9600

Gardener's Supply Company
128 Intervale Road
Burlington, VT 05401
Phone: 800-863-1700
Fax: 802-660-4600
http://www.gardeners.com

Gurney Seed & Nursery
2nd & Capital
Yankton, SD 57078
Phone: 605-665-1930

Harmony Farm Supply
P.O. Box 460
Graton, CA 95444
Phone: 707-823-9125
Fax: 707-823-1734

Harris Seeds
961 Lyell Avenue
Rochester, NY 14606
Phone: 800-514-4441

H.G. Hasting Co.
1036 White St., S.W.
Atlanta, GA 30310
Phone: 800-285-6580
Fax: 404-755-6059

Henry Fields
415 North Burnett
Shenandoah, IA 51602
Phone: 605-665-4491
Fax: 605-665-2601

Jackson & Perkins
P.O. Box 1028
2518 S. Pacific Highway
Medford, OR 97501
Phone: 800-292-4769

John Deere Catalog
1400 Third Avenue
Moline, IL 61265
Phone: 309-765-8000

Johnny's Selected Seeds
Foss Hill Road
Albion, ME 04910
Phone: 207-437-9294
Fax: 207-437-2165
http://johnnyseeds.com

J.W. Jung Seed Co.
335 S. High Street
Randolph, WI 53757
Phone: 800-247-5864

Kemp Company
160 Koser Road
Lititz, PA 17543
Phone: 717-627-7979

Kinsman Company, Inc.
River Road
Point Pleasant, PA 18950
Phone: 215-297-5613

Mellinger's Inc.
2310 W. South Range Road
N. Lima, OH 44452-9731
Phone: 216-549-9861 or
800-321-7444
http://www.mellingers.com

Modern Farm
1825 Big Horn Avenue
Cody, WY 82414
Phone: 307-587-5946

Natural Gardening Company
217 San Anselmo Avenue
San Anselmo, CA 94960
Phone: 707-766-9303
Fax: 707-766-9747

Necessary Organics
P.O. Box 305
422 Salem Avenue
New Castle, VA 24127
Phone: 540-864-5103

Plow and Hearth
301 Madison Road
Orange, VA 22960
Phone: 540-94-5412

Ringer Corporation
9959 Valley View Road
Eden Prairie, MN 55344-3585
Phone: 800-423-7544

Seventh Generation
49 The Meadows Park
Colchester, VT 05446-1672
Phone: 802-655-2700

Smith & Hawken
25 Corte Madera
Mill Valley, CA 94941
Phone: 800-776-5558

The Walt Nicke Company
P.O. Box 443
36 McLeod Lane
Topsfield, MA 01983
Phone: 800-822-4114

Biodynamic Association
P.O. Box 550
Kimberton, PA 19442
Phone: 800-516-7797

Suggested Reading

Appelhof, Mary. *Worms Eat My Garbage*. Kalamazoo, MI: Flowerfield Enterprises, 1997.

Backyard Composting: Your Complete Guide to Recycling Yard Clippings. Ojai, CA: Harmonious Technologies, 1995.

Ball, James. *Easy Composting, Environmentally Friendly Gardening*. Des Moines, IA: Meredith Books, 1993.

Beck, Malcolm. *The Secret Life of Compost: A 'How-to' & 'Why' Guide to Composting — Lawn, Garden, Feedlot, or Farm*. Metairie, LA: Acres USA, 1997.

Biocycle Guide to the Art and Science of Composting. New York: HarperCollins, 1991.

Campbell, Stu. *The Mulch Book: A Complete Guide for Gardeners*. Pownal, VT: Storey Communications, Inc., 1991.

Christopher, Tom, and Marty Asher. *Compost This Book!: The Art of Composting for Your Yard, Your Community, and the Planet*. San Francisco: Sierra Club Books, 1994.

Cullen, Mark, Lorraine Johnson, and Andrew Leyerle. *The Urban/Suburban Composter: The Complete Guide to Backyard, Balcony, and Apartment Composting*. New York: St. Martin's Press, 1994.

Foster, Catherine Osgood. *Building Healthy Gardens: A Safe and Natural Approach*. Pownal, VT: Storey Communications, Inc., 1989.

Hunter, Beatrice Trum. *Gardening Without Poisons*. Boston: Houghton Mifflin, 1964.

Martin, Deborah L., and Grace Gershuny, editors. *The Rodale Book of Composting*. Emmaus, PA: Rodale Press, Inc., 1992.

Parnes, Robert. *Fertile Soil: A Grower's Guide to Organic & Inorganic Fertilizers*. Davis, CA: Ag Access, 1990.

Soloman, Steve. *Organic Gardener's Composting*. Washougal, WA: Van Patten Publishers, 1993.

Index

Other Storey Titles You Will Enjoy

The Big Book of Gardening Secrets, by Charles W.G. Smith. Provides scores of professional secrets for growing better vegetables, herbs, fruits, and flowers. 352 pages. Paperback. ISBN 1-58017-000-5.

Carrots Love Tomatoes, by Louise Riotte. Explains how to put vegetable relationships to work for you in your garden to produce a bountiful crop. Contains hundreds of interesting facts that offer practical advice and entertaining reading. 224 pages. Paperback. ISBN 1-58017-027-7.

Green Thumb Wisdom, by Doc and Katy Abraham. Provides valuable facts and tips on houseplants, flowers, vegetables, fruits and berries, watering, insects, soil, compost, mulch, fertilizers, and much more. 144 pages. Paperback. ISBN 0-88266-928-1.

The Mulch Book, by Stu Campbell. Details how to use bark, stones, hay, compost, plastic sheeting, and other materials as a barrier for keeping weeds out and beneficial elements in. 160 pages. Paperback. ISBN 0-88266-659-2.

The Organic Gardener's Home Reference, by Tonya Denckla. Includes complete information for growing, harvesting, and storing 62 of the most popular vegetables, fruits, nuts, and herbs. 304 pages. Paperback. ISBN 0-88266-839-0.

Secrets to Great Soil, by Elizabeth P. Stell. Shows how soil health affects gardens, and how to evaluate your soil's texture, structure, pH, and general fertility. 224 pages. Hardcover. ISBN 1-58017-009-9.

Tips For the Lazy Gardener, by Linda Tilgner. Contains hundreds of valuable suggestions for every gardener who wants to cut down on weeding and enjoy gardening more. 144 pages. Paperback. ISBN 1-58017-026-9.

These books and other Storey books are available at your bookstore, farm store, garden center, or directly from Storey Publishing, Schoolhouse Road, Pownal, Vermont 05261, or by calling 1-800-441-5700. www.storey.com.